First World War
and Army of Occupation
War Diary
France, Belgium and Germany

50 DIVISION
Divisional Troops
Royal Irish Regiment
5th Battalion Pioneers
1 April 1918 - 28 February 1919

WO95/2823/1

The Naval & Military Press Ltd
www.nmarchive.com
Published in association with The National Archives

Published by

The Naval & Military Press Ltd

Unit 10 Ridgewood Industrial Park,

Uckfield, East Sussex,

TN22 5QE England

Tel: +44 (0) 1825 749494

www.naval-military-press.com

www.nmarchive.com

This diary has been reprinted in facsimile from the original. Any imperfections are inevitably reproduced and the quality may fall short of modern type and cartographic standards.

© **Crown Copyright**
Images reproduced by permission of The National Archives, London, England, 2015.

Contents

Document type	Place/Title	Date From	Date To
Heading	WO95/2823 50 Div 5/R. Irish (Pioneers) Apr 18-Feb 19		
Heading	50th Division 5th Bn Royal Irish Regt (Pioneers) Apl 1918-Feb 1919 From Egypt 10 Divl Troops To 2 Div Troops		
Heading	52nd Division 1-5th Bn Roy. Irish Regt (Pioneers) Apr-May 1918		
Heading	52nd Divisional Pioneers Disembarked Marseilles from Egypt 17.4.18. 1/5th Battalion Royal Irish Regiment (Pioneers) April 1918		
War Diary	Palestine (Birzeit)	01/04/1918	06/04/1918
War Diary	Palestine (Kantara)	07/04/1918	08/04/1918
War Diary	Egypt (Kantara) (Alexandria)	08/04/1918	11/04/1918
War Diary	Mediterranean	12/04/1918	16/04/1918
War Diary	France (Marseilles)	17/04/1918	20/04/1918
War Diary	France	21/04/1918	21/04/1918
War Diary	Hautvillers	22/04/1918	27/04/1918
War Diary	France (Hautvillers)	28/04/1918	30/04/1918
War Diary	Sheet (in the case of attached officers)	30/04/1918	30/04/1918
War Diary	Monchester Regt.	30/04/1918	30/04/1918
War Diary	Royal Jersey Mils	30/04/1918	30/04/1918
Heading	War Diary of 5th (S) Battalion Royal Irish Regiment (Pioneers) From 1st May 1918 to 31st May 1918 (Volume 35)		
War Diary	France	01/05/1918	31/05/1918
Miscellaneous		31/05/1918	31/05/1918
Heading	War Diary of 5th (Service) Bn Royal Irish Regt. (Pioneers) from 1st June 1918 to 30th June 1918 (Volume 36)		
War Diary	France	01/06/1918	30/06/1918
Miscellaneous	5th (S) Battalion Royal Irish Regiment (Pioneers)	30/06/1918	30/06/1918
Heading	War Diary of 5th Bn Royal Irish Regt (Pioneers) From 1st July 1918 to 31st July 1918 (Volume 37)		
War Diary	France	01/07/1918	31/07/1918
Miscellaneous	5th (S) Battalion Royal Irish Regiment (Pioneers)	31/07/1918	31/07/1918
Heading	War Diary of 5th Bn Royal Irish Rgt (Pioneers) from 1st August 1918 to 31st August 1918 Volume 38		
War Diary	France	01/08/1918	31/08/1918
Miscellaneous	5th (S) Battalion Royal Irish Regiment (Pioneers)		
Heading	War Diary of 5th Bn Royal Irish Regiment (Pioneers) from 1st September 1918 to 30th September 1918 Volume 39		
War Diary	France	01/09/1918	30/09/1918
Miscellaneous	5th (S) Battalion Royal Irish Regiment (Pioneers)	30/09/1918	30/09/1918
Heading	War Diary of 5th Bn Royal Irish Regt. (Pioneers) From 1st October 1918 to 31st October 1918 Volume 40		
War Diary	France	01/10/1918	31/10/1918
Miscellaneous		31/10/1918	31/10/1918
Heading	War Diary of 5th Bn Royal Irish Regt. (Pioneers) From 1st November 1918 to 30th November 1918 Volume 41.		

War Diary Miscellaneous	France	01/11/1918	30/11/1918
Heading	War Diary of 5th Bn Royal Irish Regiment (Pioneers) From 1st December 1918 to 31st December 1918 Volume 42		
War Diary Miscellaneous	France	01/12/1918 31/12/1918	31/12/1918 31/12/1918
Heading	War Diary of 5th Bn Royal Irish Rgt. (Pioneers) From 1st January 1919 to 31st January 1919 Volume 43		
War Diary Miscellaneous	France	01/01/1919	31/01/1919
Heading	War Diary of 5th Bn Royal Irish Regt (Pioneers) From 1st February 1919 to 28th February 1919 Volume 44		
War Diary Miscellaneous	France St. Waast La Vallee	01/02/1919 28/02/1919	28/02/1919 28/02/1919

WO95/2823
50 Div
5/ R. Irish (Pioneers)
Apr '18 - Feb '19

50TH DIVISION

**5TH BN ROYAL IRISH REGT
(PIONEERS)
APL ~~JAN~~ 1918-FEB 1919**

FROM EGYPT 10 DIV' TROOPS

TO 2 DIV TROOPS

52ND DIVISION

1-5TH BN ROY. IRISH REGT
(PIONEERS)
APR-MAY 1916

52nd Divisional Pioneers

Disembarked MARSEILLES from EGYPT 17.4.18.

1/5th BATTALION

ROYAL IRISH REGIMENT (Pioneers)

APRIL 1918.

Army Form C. 2118.

WAR DIARY

INTELLIGENCE SUMMARY. Page 1.

(Erase heading not required.)

5th (S) BATTALION ROYAL IRISH REGIMENT (PIONEERS)

Place	Date	Hour	Summary of Events and Information	Remarks and references to Appendices
PALESTINE (BIRZEIT)	1918. April 1		B" left BIRZEIT (PALESTINE Sheet 14, M.7.B.) enroute to join 52nd (Lowland) Division on transfer. Camped for night at IBN HARITH (Sheet 14, F.25)	NIL
	" 2		B" marched to LATRON, and camped for night	NIL
	" 3		B" marched to SARAFEND near LUDD, and joined with 52nd (Lowland) Division.	NIL
	" 4		B" halted at SARAFEND. Time spent on renewing equipment and clothing of B". Small Box Respirators drawn, fitted and tested by each officer and man going through Gas tent.	NIL
	" 5		Regimental Transport, Officers riding horses, and all equipment special to E.E.F. handed over to the Departments concerned, in view of the B" proceeding to another Front.	NIL
	" 6		B" paraded at 2330 and marched to LUDD Railway Station to entrain for KANTARA EAST	NIL
PALESTINE (KANTARA)	" 7		B" entrained and left at 0300. Arrived KANTARA EAST at 1839 and marched to No. 2 Infantry Base Depot Camp for accommodation for the night	

Strength Return for week ending 7th April

	O	OR
Effective Strength	24	815
Ration Strength	26	816
	0	16
	1	16
	-	22

Admitted to HOSPITAL
Rejoined from hospital, etc.

2nd Lieut J.W. Day was admitted to Hospital from School of Instruction ZEITOUN

Army Form C. 2118.

WAR DIARY
or
INTELLIGENCE SUMMARY. Page 2.

6th (S) BATTALION ROYAL IRISH REGIMENT (F. OFFICERS)

(Erase heading not required.)

Place	Date 1918	Hour	Summary of Events and Information	Remarks and references to Appendices
PALESTINE (KANTARA)	April 8		88 O.R. reinforcements (men from leave, classes of instruction, hospital etc.) joined from No 2 Infantry Base Depot. Bn paraded at 1630 and marched - crossing SUEZ CANAL by Bridge - to KANTARA WEST to entrain for Alexandria.	HWL
EGYPT (KANTARA)	" "		Bn entrained at KANTARA WEST and left at 2050 for Alexandria	HWL
(ALEXANDRIA)	" 9		Bn arrived at ALEXANDRIA at 0540. As the Transport Vessel for the Bn was not ready instructions were received to detrain and proceed to SIDI BISHR Camp for accommodation. Stayed the day and night.	HWL
	" 10		Bn entrained at SIDI BISHR Siding at 1315 and proceeded to DOCKS Siding, where the Bn embarked during the afternoon on H.M.T. "CALEDONIA" Strength 32 Officers, 682 Other Ranks.	HWL
	" 11		"CALEDONIA" in harbour. No 2091 Private W. CLYNE B.Coy., an absentee from embarkation on 10th was brought on board increasing the strength of O.R. to 683. Sailed at 1500.	HWL HWL HWL
MEDITERRANEAN	" 12		At Sea	
	" 13		At Sea	

Strength Return for date of sailing and week ending 13th April. 1

	O.	O.R.
Effective Strength	30	682	Admitted to Hospital etc
Ration Strength	32	683	Rejoined from hospital etc
	0	0
	"	3
	6	69

Major R.F. STEPHEN joined on 10th from Hospital. Major G.W. HAWKES, met Capt G. HARDING, who had been on Sick Base joined the Bn. Also 2nd Lieuts R. HEALY and E. GREER from School of Instructors, ZEITOUN and 2nd Lieut McRAE.

Army Form C. 2118.

WAR DIARY
— or —
INTELLIGENCE SUMMARY. page 3

(Erase heading not required.)

5th (S) BATTALION ROYAL IRISH REGIMENT (PIONEERS)

Instructions regarding War Diaries and Intelligence Summaries are contained in F. S. Regs., Part II. and the Staff Manual respectively. Title pages will be prepared in manuscript.

Place	Date	Hour	Summary of Events and Information	Remarks and references to Appendices
	1918			
MEDITERRANEAN	April 14		At Sea. Divine Service held	Nil
	" 15		At Sea.	Nil
	" 16		At Sea	
	" 17		"CALEDONIA" reached MARSEILLES at 10 a.m. disembarkation of Bn. completed at 1 p.m. Bn. then marched to CARCASSONE Rest Camp for accommodation. No casualties during voyage. So strength of Bn. did not vary —	Nil
FRANCE (MARSEILLES)			Strength of Bn. on disembarkation	
			O OR	
			Effective Strength 30 682	
			Ration Strength 32 683	
	" 18		Bn. at CARCASSONE Camp. Paraded at 1 p.m. and marched to Railway Station. Entrained at 4.39 p.m. and left Marseilles.	Nil
	" 19		Bn. in train	Nil
	" 20		Bn. in train	Nil
			Strength Return for week ending 20th April	
			O OR	
			Effective Strength 29 654	
			Ration Strength 31 855	
			O OR	
			Admitted to Hospital etc 0 28	
			Rejoined from Hospital etc 1 —	
			2nd Lieut J. HUGLIN admitted to hospital on HMT "CALEDONIA", and transferred to Hospital in MARSEILLES	Nil

Army Form C. 2118.

WAR DIARY
or
INTELLIGENCE SUMMARY. Page 4.

5th (S) BATTALION ROYAL IRISH REGIMENT (PIONEERS)

(Erase heading not required.)

Instructions regarding War Diaries and Intelligence Summaries are contained in F. S. Regs., Part II. and the Staff Manual respectively. Title pages will be prepared in manuscript.

Place	Date	Hour	Summary of Events and Information	Remarks and references to Appendices
	1918			
FRANCE	April 21		B'n train. Reached NOYELLES Station at 10.30 a.m., detrained and marched to village of HAUTVILLERS where B'n billeted.	Nil
HAUTVILLERS	" 22		Settled down in billets.	Nil
	" 23		Commenced refresher training, especially Gas Drill. Received over Regtl Transport (part) on the scale for "Pioneer B'n" (FRANCE)	Nil
	" 24		Training carried on.	Nil
	" 25		Under authority of W.O. letter No. 121/France/1568 (S.D.2), and the revised establishment for a Pioneer B'n, received from H.Q. 52nd Division, the B'n was reorganised on the 3 Coy System. "B" Coy (Commander Capt E.C. BEARD) was split up, and the present "D" Coy (Commander Major E.F.STEPHEN) becomes "B" Coy.	Nil
	" 26		three hours The Corps Gas Officer gave a lecture on GAS to the B'n	
	" 27		Strength Return for week ending 27th April	
			O. O.R.	
			Effective Strength 30 832	
			Ration Strength 35 836	
				O. O.R.
			Admitted to hospital 0 23	
			Rejoined from hospital - 1	Nil
			2nd Lieut J HUELIN rejoined on 25th from hospital.	

Army Form C. 2118.

WAR DIARY
or
INTELLIGENCE SUMMARY. Page 5.
(Erase heading not required.)

5th (S) BATTALION ROYAL IRISH REGIMENT (PIONEERS)

Instructions regarding War Diaries and Intelligence
Summaries are contained in F. S. Regs., Part II.
and the Staff Manual respectively. Title pages
will be prepared in manuscript.

Place	Date	Hour	Summary of Events and Information	Remarks and references to Appendices
FRANCE (HAUTVILLERS)	1918 April 28		Sunday. HOLIDAY. Divine Service for R.C's.	Nil
	" 29		B" ordered to move to AIRE. "A" and "B" Coys under Major G.W. HAWKES. M.C. entrained at NOYELLES Station at 0900, detrained at BERGUETTE Station at 1900, and marched to AIRE, and were put up in the French Cavalry Barracks, officers being billeted in town. Remainder of B" (H.Qrs and "C" Coy) entrained at NOYELLES at 1900	Nil
	" 30		B" H.Qrs and "C" Coy detrained at BERGUETTE Station at 0600 marched to AIRE. Men billeted (with "A" and "D" Coys) in the French Cavalry Barracks, and Officers in town.	Nil

H.W.Cunningham, Captain,
Adjutant 5th (S) Bn. The Royal Irish Regt.
(Pioneers)

Army Form C. 2118.

WAR DIARY
or
INTELLIGENCE SUMMARY. page 6.

5th (S) BATTALION ROYAL IRISH REGIMENT (PIONEERS)

Instructions regarding War Diaries and Intelligence Summaries are contained in F.S. Regs., Part II. and the Staff Manual respectively. Title pages will be prepared in manuscript. *Effective State of Bn. for 30th April 1918.* (Erase heading not required.)

Place	Date	Hour	Summary of Events and Information					Remarks and references to Appendices
			Roll of Officers				Present state	
		Rank	Name		Unit	Appoint		O	OR
(see the name of Attached Officers)	Comdg	Lt.Col	CROGAN	D.S.O. G.M.	(Table one of Attached) Black Watch (T.F.)		Effectives	30	798
	2nd in Comd	Major	HAWKES M.C.	G.W.	do		Attached on Establishment	2	1
	Comdg B	Captain	STEPHEN	E.F.	Royal Munster Fus.	Asst. Adjt.	Attached for rations	-	-
	A	"	FOLEY	G.R.F.	do				
	C	"	HARDING	G.	do	Lewis Guns			
		"	BEARD	E.C.	Royal Irish Regt.		Total	32	799
		"	HENDRY	W.	do				
		"	JONES	A.I.W.	do			13th attached
Manchester Road		Lieut	DAWSON M.V.O.	G.St.		Actg Q.M.	Riding horses	10	
			ARMSTRONG	A.			Draught horses	56	
			BAILLIE	W.B.			Pack horses	12	
			McRAE	T.A.N.			Lewis Guns	8	
			BRODERICK	W.F.	R.A.M.C.		Pack machine guns	12	
	Transport		ROCHE	M.L.	Chaplains Dept.	Armoured Off.	G.S. Wagons	6	
	Signalling		ROSS	H.R.		R.C. Chaplain	G.S. Limber wagons	7	
	Gas Officer		MALCOMSON	A.			Field Kitchens	3	
			LOWE	A.			Water Carts	2	
			HUFLIN	J.			Machine Carts	1	
							Maxim wagons		
Royal Irish Rifle		2nd Lieut	FERGUSON	A.K.			Lewis Carts	1	
			GREER	E.			Bicycles	10	

				Rank	Name			
				2nd Lieut	BURT	R.D.		
				"	CARNEGIE	R.Y.		
				"	EGAN	T.J.		
				"	HEALY	E.		
				"	McNALLY	F.J.		
				"	BELL	W.J.		
				"	McCAUSLAND	J.		
				"	WYLIE	J.		
				"	CLARE	J.		
				Captain	CUNNINGHAM	H.V.		
				Lieut	SULLIVAN	J.		
				Rev. Father C.F.4th Cl.	O'FARRELL Mc	R		

ORIGINAL

CONFIDENTIAL

WAR DIARY

of

5th (S) BATTALION ROYAL IRISH REGIMENT (PIONEERS)

From 1st May 1918 to 31st May 1918

(Volume 35)

WAR DIARY or INTELLIGENCE SUMMARY

Army Form C. 2118.

5th (S) BATTALION ROYAL IRISH REGIMENT (PIONEERS)

PAGE 1

Place	Date	Hour	Summary of Events and Information	Remarks and references to Appendices
FRANCE	May 1918			
	1st	—	Bn. moved from AIRE to THIENNES, Hd Qrs leading at 8 am. Coys following at 15 mins interval. Arriving about 10 am. Embussed on Forest de NIEPPE (SP.P.O) Sheet HAZEBROUCK 5A. Reconnm. instructors returned to their Units. C.O. & Coy Command. and Coy Commanders met the C.R.E. 5 Div at THIENNES at 9 am to be shewn position where Bn. should work.	JG
	2nd		Coys marched off by Platoons at 4.30 am to work on new line of defence from D 28 a.a. to J 24 central (sheet 36A) Coy went met Rly and gave all day meal 10 min in work. About 300 shovels from R.E. Dump Sn. Div. Coys returned to camp about 5 pm. A small party worked all day improving Camp. Xero for Coys on return to camp.	JG
	3rd		Coys carried on with work as previous day. C.O. 2nd in Command A/C and O/c A & B Coys attended a lecture on "Recent Operations" given by Hall AIRE from 3 pm to 6 pm. Two Platoons of A Coy found working party during afternoon.	JG
	4th		Coys worked as yesterday. All HdQrs attended at Gas Hut at 10 am. Remainder of A Coy went to Thithus h at 3 pm. Strength Return for week ending Saturday 4th May 1918. Effective 30 O. Y35 O.R. admitted to Hosp. 23 O.R. Ration 32 O. Y38 O.R. Rejoined from Hosp —	JG

WAR DIARY
INTELLIGENCE SUMMARY

5th (S) BATTALION ROYAL IRISH REGIMENT (PIONEERS)

PAGE II

Army Form C. 2118.

Place	Date	Hour	Summary of Events and Information	Remarks and references to Appendices
FRANCE	May 1918 5th		Raining all night and morning. Church Parade held in THIENNES Church at 8:30 am. R.C. Service was arranged at in the life to allow of all B[n] getting. Transport with all baggage loaded up by 9 a.m. At 10:30 am C[o]ys sent out working parties through the Gas Hill. O.M & Q.M Sergt joined the Div. Column at AIRE and remained the night at DIVION Bn and 3 C.O.M Sergts proceeded to Mont St ELOI. Riding Party and wire conveyed by lorry to MONT ST ELOI.	✗
	6th		B[n] marched to AIRE at 8:45 am and left march H.Q. A B & C Coys (100+ arrived between 6.9.3) arrived in Syphone by Artillery Barracks about 12 midday, all attended a lecture in the Barracks from R.T.O by Colonel Campbell from 12.30 to 1.30 am. Cooking Utensils and luggage brought up by lorry arrived at behind men had dinners on the Square at 5.30 pm marched to Station and had tea. At 10:30 pm entrained at AIRE spending the night in the train.	✗
	7th		Arrived at ACQ Station at 4 am. Detrained and was met by C.O. in Sigs who guided Battalion to new billeting Area at Mont St Eloi. on arrival conveyed all baggage from Station to Camp. 10 Officers and 30 O.R. were left behind as unloading party. B[n] arrived at Mess Camp (Nab) at 8:45 am and was immediately given breakfast. Unloading party arrived about 10:30 am the morning heavily all morning cleaning up. About mid-day.	✗

Army Form C. 2118.

WAR DIARY
or
INTELLIGENCE SUMMARY.

(Erase heading not required.) PAGE III

6th (S) BATTALION ROYAL IRISH REGIMENT (PIONEERS)

Place	Date	Hour	Summary of Events and Information	Remarks and references to Appendices
FRANCE	May 1918			
	8th		Morning devoted to Gas training and training of Signallers. Afternoon bathing and washing. 1 Sergt and 91 OR proceeded to Div Salvage Coy at Aux Rietz.	
	9th		Coys paraded at 6am (fighting order with tools) and marched off by coys at 300x interval to work Thieslipeing TIRED ALLEY At QM and Transport moved to NEUVILLE ST VAAST at 9am arriving at 11am, turned its billets (camp huts) Transport cannot Coys paces. Coys arrived in new camp about 8.30 pm.	
	10th		Coys marched out of camp at 9 am to continue work on TIRED ALLEY C Coy shelled with Gas and H.E. shells during the afternoon. 1 OR Engr gassed. Lieut J SULLIVAN M.O. was wounded. All Coys completed days work R by 4.30 PM and returned to Camp. 1 Platoon of C Coy paraded at 10 PM for work on TIRED ALLEY during the night, returning to Camp at 4.30 am. Pte Calvert granted 14 days Special Leave to Gtd U.K.	
	11th		The Coys during the day. A day holiday. Special Items granted to all @w 3 O.R. A Coy and 30 O.R. C Coy from 11 am to 12 noon proceeded to U.K. 80 OR A Coy and 30 O.R. worked on Bde H.Q. at PETITE VIMY. C Coy under Lauriston Kenley Coys worked all night wiring TIRED ALLEY during the night R and C from the RE Dump Z IVY batt J Mitchell wiring Lapon ets otherwise Sunday Return for Week ending Saturday 11th May 1918. Admitted to Hospital 35 OR Strength 31 O 680 OR Establish 30 O 689 OR Bayonets from Hospital 6 Ration 31 O 690 OR	

WAR DIARY
INTELLIGENCE SUMMARY. 5th (9) BATTALION ROYAL IRISH REGIMENT (PIONEERS)

PAGE IV

Place	Date	Hour	Summary of Events and Information	Remarks and references to Appendices
FRANCE	May 1918			
	12th		R.C. Service at 10 am in Cinema Hut - LE TARGETTE. 3 O.R. B Coy. have 14 U.K. Captain Harding and party worked as yesterday night. also B & C Coys were shelled before entering the trench and Private L. Roach C. Coy was killed. 1 O.R. wounded from bomb at Cinema Hut watching him.	JFC
	13th		Capt. Foley and Capt. Beard met C.R.E. at 155 Bde H.Q. at 9 am to be shown their work. Private J. Roach was buried at LETARGETTE Cemetery. A & B Coys worked during night on FARBUS line making a S.P. C Coy & Pioneers Brown line. Lieut. Dawson M.V.O. to Hospital. 3 O.R. C Coy on leave 14 U.K.	JFC
	14th		3 O.R. B.H.Q. on leave to U.K. Work for day same as previous night. All transport animals under Inspection isolation within range.	JFC
	15th		G.O.C. inspected B.H.Q. and interviewed the C.O. 3 O.R. on leave to U.K. Captain Fraser Connaught Rangers and Lieut. Godfrey 2nd R.I. Regt. joined and posted to B. Coy & Sergeant from same Bns accompanied Lt Godfrey. Coys working as previous night.	JFC
	16th		Captain Harding to Div. H.Q. to practice Staff duties. Captain Henry took over Command of C. Coy. 3 O.R. B Coy on leave Eng'd. worked as previous night. Enemy Aeroplane fired on A & B Coy about 10.30 p.m. No casualties. Lieut. Mullin to Hospital.	JFC
	17th		Captain Jones and 2 O.R. C Coy on leave to U.K. Coys continued work as usual. A & B Coys on FARBUS S.P. and C Coy on BROWN line.	JFC

WAR DIARY
INTELLIGENCE SUMMARY.
5th (8) BATTALION ROYAL IRISH REGIMENT (PIONEERS)

Army Form C. 2118.

Place	Date	Hour	Summary of Events and Information	Remarks and references to Appendices
FRANCE	May 1918			
	18th		Captain Beard went to Commandant House ( ) at 3pm to be shown work for night. by Major Billings OC 412 F.C. RE. Coys then worked as usual. Shelled during night and 1 man C Coy slightly wounded. Gas instruction on gas bombs at XVIII Corps Gas School. 3 O.R. Transport Leave TUR given by 5/6 (Highland) Divn. attended a demonstration at ECOUVIERS.	
			Effective Strength for week ending Saturday 11th May 1918	
			E. Officers 28 0 639 O.R. attached to Corps 5 8 T.O.R	
			E. Officers 30 0 W.O 1 O.R. Returned from Hosp 8 O.R.	
			Ration	
	19th		Voluntary R.C. Service in Cinema LATARGETTE at 10am. Sergt Hughes on PORT 'Course. A Coy worked during night unloading huts. Spuds for R.E. near 15/ 13/c N.O. B Coy on FARBUS DUMP. C Coy on Roads Line. C Coy carried to Roads in R.E. S Waggons and back again.	
			3 O.R. A Coy on leave to UK.	
	20th		3 O.R. B Coy on leave to UK. 2/Lieut Carnegie to Div on Light Railway work. Coys worked as above nights. Lieut 1 Platoon B Coy under Lieut Rowe.	
	21st		Major Skipton and 30 O.R. C Coy on leave. at 6am Lieut Rowe and 10 OR went to work on tunnel under road at FARBUS S.P. and clearing from TB to C Coy. Coys worked as yesterday. T.O. 4 Sergt attended lecture at Div Train on Mules with returners.	

WAR DIARY
INTELLIGENCE SUMMARY.

Army Form C. 2118.

5th (S) BATTALION ROYAL IRISH REGIMENT (PIONEERS)

PAGE VI

Place	Date	Hour	Summary of Events and Information	Remarks and references to Appendices
FRANCE	May 1918			
	22nd		6 Coy worked on FARBUS S.P. from 2 am until mid-day. G.S. Waggons conveying them to and from work. 3 OR HO on leave to UK. Rest down to rifle. A & B Coys as yesterday.	
	23rd		6 Coy had to return from work at 6 am owing to Geo Shelling. Went out again at 11.30 am and worked until 4.30 pm. A & B Coys as usual. 33 men joined from England via Infantry Base Depot. 3 OR A Coy on leave to UK. Lieut. Ferguson to Hospital.	
	24th		Raining heavily all morning up to mid-day. Lieut McRae and A/CSM Nolan to this Rifle course. Hy Coy then D.O.R. 73 Cpl and OR C Coy on leave to UK. All on and to Hospital. B and C Coy worked during night in FARBUS S.P. C and A Coys exchanging jobs of work. C Coy making a.c.T. from S.P. to THELUS. A Coy working on BROWN LINE from 4 am 4.30 pm. 2 Lt E Greer took over District Commandant of NEUVILLE ST VAAST. 18 OR returned from Div Salvage Coy. 6 OR to Divl. Carriage for light Railway work. B & C Coys. worked in last night.	
	25th		2 Lt. who to Hospital. Lieut Love partly completed tunnel. Effective Strength for Week ending Saturday 25th May 1918. Effective 226 604 OR admitted to Hospital 5 52 OR Ration 240 606 OR Reported from Hospt. 5	

Army Form C. 2118.

WAR DIARY
or
INTELLIGENCE SUMMARY

(Erase heading not required.) PAGE VII

5th (S) BATTALION ROYAL IRISH REGIMENT (PIONEERS)

Instructions regarding War Diaries and Intelligence Summaries are contained in F. S. Regs., Part II. and the Staff Manual respectively. Title pages will be prepared in manuscript.

Place	Date	Hour	Summary of Events and Information	Remarks and references to Appendices
FRANCE	May 1918			
	26th		Voluntary R.C. Service on terrace at 10 am. A Coy worked as usual. also B & C Coys. Lt Col W. Brown in Gas Course Lt Malcomson from Gas Course. 2n.5. Lieut. V. Nunton joined from ETAPLES and posted to C Coy.	
	27th		FARBUS shelled with Gas shells at 3am. A & C Coys continued working as usual. B. Coy couldn't work owing to position being shelled with mustard Gas.	
	28th		30th A Coy on leave A Coy went to hospital as usual at 9am. Major G.H. Manutes M.C. was presented D.F. & C.M. at Fort George. Lieut. Errington returned from hospital. Lt Malcomson on leave. N.C.Os attended a demonstration on enemy Gas at Div Gas Hut at 10.30 am. B and C Coys worked as usual.	
	29th		Batt. Sunday and 28th b. lay on leave. Lieut. Godfrey took over command of C Coy. Coys. working as previous day	
	30th		No work. day devoted to cleaning up. 3 G.S. Waggons with tools proceeded to Mont St Eloi Station. Clothing received from Div Baths	

WAR DIARY
or
INTELLIGENCE SUMMARY.

(Erase heading not required.) PAGE VIII 5th (S) BATTALION ROYAL IRISH REGIMENT (PIONEERS)

Army Form C. 2118.

Place	Date	Hour	Summary of Events and Information	Remarks and references to Appendices
FRANCE	May 1918 31st		Moved off transport and loading party of 2 officers and 50 O.R.'s 3 Coy moved off to Mont St Éloi at 8 am and commenced loading en. Medically on arrival B⁺ moved off by Platoons at 10 am arriving at Station at mid-day, when they entrained. Draft of 30 O.R. joined and leave parties from A, B & C Coys. + 4 S.H⁺ Gunns ant 8 hours joined from Oar train. Lieut. Col G M Grogan D.S.O. handed to 11th (Garr) Bn. (Pioneers) Cheshires on transfer. Major E.W Hunter M.C. took over temporary command of the Bn. Ytrain moved off at 13.15 hours arriving at Harlington Station at 10.15 pm and Camps off for the night at Dublin Rest Camp. Transport Waggons remained on the train for the night.	JK

Hy Egan M Foy / Captain
Adjutant 5th (S) Bn. The Royal Irish Regt.
(Pioneers)

Army Form C. 2118.

WAR DIARY
or
INTELLIGENCE SUMMARY.

6th (S) BATTALION ROYAL IRISH REGIMENT (PIONEERS)

(Erase heading not required.) PAGE IX

Instructions regarding War Diaries and Intelligence Summaries are contained in F. S. Regs., Part II. and the Staff Manual respectively. Title pages will be prepared in manuscript. *Fighting State of Bn. for 31st May 1918*

Place	Date	Hour	Summary of Events and Information			Remarks and references to Appendices
			UNIT	RANK	NAME	
In the trench attached officers		Comdg. Lt Col	GROGAN	DSO	G.M.	O OR
						27 628
2nd in comd		Major	HAWKES	MC	G.W.	3.
Coy A		Capt	FOLEY		G.R.E.	5
" B		"	BEARD	MC	E.C.	
A.S.C. attached Commandt. Officer		"	FRASER		A.G.C.	
		Lieut	ERRINGTON		E	
		"	ARMSTRONG		A	Present state
		"	BAILLIE		N.B.	34 634
		"	BRODERICK		N.F.	8 attached
		"	ROCHE		M.L	
Signalling		"	ROSS		H.E	Total
		"	MALCOMSON		A	8"
		"	LONE		A	Riding Horses 10
		"	GODFREY		P.J	Draught Horses 53
Comdg C.Of.		2/Lt	HUNTER		V	Pack Horses 12
		"	EGAN		T.J	Lewis Guns 12
Reg. transport. Transport.		"	HEALY		F	Pack Saddlery (sets) 13
		"	McNALLY		F.J	G.S.Waggons 6
" "	Transport	"	BELL		W.T.	G.S.Limbers 4
" "		"	WYLIE		J	Field Kitchens 3
	Q.Comm.d.	"	CLARE		J	Water Carts 2
Adjt.		A/Capt	CUNNINGHAM		H.U.	Malkatcarts 1
						Mess Carts 1
						Bicycles 10

Unit	Rank	Name
R.A.M.C	Medical Officer	Captain MITCHELL T.M. Effective
Chaplains Dept.	R.C. Chaplain Revd Father O'FARRELL C.F. ws Glass	P. Attached on Estab
		attached for Rations

Original

— CONFIDENTIAL —

WAR DIARY
of
5^{s} (Service) Bn Royal Irish Regt. (Pioneers)

from 1st June 1918 to 30^{s} June 1918

(Volume 36)

Army Form C. 2118.

WAR DIARY
or
INTELLIGENCE SUMMARY.

(Erase heading not required.) PAGE 1

5th (S) BATTALION ROYAL IRISH REGIMENT (PIONEERS)

Place	Date	Hour	Summary of Events and Information	Remarks and references to Appendices
FRANCE	June 1918			
	1st		Transport unloaded from train at 6 a.m. Battn moved to TARDINGHEN at 10.30 a.m by companies. One lorry carried out all mens packs and tools and then drew rations from SLACK RAILHEAD. 2/Lt Grogan went to ETAPLES to take over command of 11th Garn Bn Pioneers. Lt Ross to Hospital. DSO Strength Return for week ending Saturday 1st June 1918 Effective 21 O 628 O.R. Admitted to Hospital 44 O.R Ration 23 O 634 O.R. Rejoined from Hospital 39 O.R	
	2nd		R.C. Service in village Church at 9 a.m. Holiday. Capt Jones from leave. 1 O.R 'B' Coy on leave. Lt Armstrong to Hoaths	
	3rd		Coys carried out Section Training all morning. Bathing and Recreational games during afternoon. 2 O.R 'C' Company on leave	
	4th		Coys training as usual. Football matches and bathing during afternoon. 1 O.R 'A' Coy. 1 OR 'B' Coy on leave. Lt King and Lt Breedon joined. Lt McCausland from Hospital. Football match at 6 p.m between H.Q and Transport. Boys carried on training as usual. Disinfector arrived from Base to 2. 2 O.R.C. Coy on leave.	
	5th		Coys training as usual. Clothing of H.Q. and Transport disinfected 1 O.R 'A' on leave.	
	6th		Capt. Davis and Lt. Sloan and Devany joined 1 O.R 'B' Coy on leave.	
	7th		Training as usual	

WAR DIARY
INTELLIGENCE SUMMARY.

Army Form C. 2118.

(Erase heading not required.) PAGE 2

5th (S) BATTALION ROYAL IRISH REGIMENT (PIONEERS)

Place	Date	Hour	Summary of Events and Information	Remarks and references to Appendices
FRANCE	MAY 1918			
	8th		Comdg Officer inspected kits and billets of Bn at 9 am. Training as usual. 1 OR "B" Coy, 1 OR "C" Coy on leave. Strength Return for week ending Saturday June 8th Effective 26 O. 619 OR. Admitted to hospital 23 O/R. Ration 28 O. 628 OR. Rejoined from hospital 20 O/R. Lt McCarthy, Lt North and 16 OR joined. Lt Barry and 1 OR "A" Coy on leave.	✓
	9th		Holiday. R.C. Service in Church at 10 am. R.C. Service at 5 pm. 1 OR "A" Coy on leave.	✓
	10th		Raining heavily all morning. Lt Meehan joined. Coys paraded in billets. Capt Davis and Jones went to inspect work to be done at AUDRESSELLES. 1 OR "A" Coy, 1 OR "B" Coy on leave.	✓
	11th		"C" Coy moved to AUDRESSELLES at 2 pm. Capt Hamilton and 25 OR joined. A & B Coys training as usual. Football during afternoon. 2 OR "C" Coy on leave.	✓
	12th		Coys training as usual. C.O. inspected kits and billets of "A" Coy at 10 am. Capt Beard and 1 O/R "A" Coy on leave.	✓
	13th		Coys training as usual. C.O. inspected kits and billets of "B" Coy at 10 am. 1 O/R "B" Coy on leave.	✓
	14th		Coys training as usual. C.O. inspected kits and billets of H.Q. at 11 am. 1 O/R "C" Coy on leave.	✓

WAR DIARY
or
INTELLIGENCE SUMMARY.

(Erase heading not required.) Page 3   6th (S) BATTALION ROYAL IRISH REGIMENT (PIONEERS)

Army Form C. 2118.

Place	Date	Hour	Summary of Events and Information	Remarks and references to Appendices
FRANCE	June 1918			
	15th		Lieut Ross from Hospital. A & B Coys had route march during morning. 1 O/R "B" Coy and 1 O/R "C" Coy on leave. Strength Return for week ending Saturday 15th June 1918. Effective 29 O 661 OR Admitted to Hosp 21 O/R Ration 31 O 666 OR Rejoined from Hosp 41 O/R	96
	16th		R.C. Service in Church at 10am for A & B Coys. HQ and Transport. O & C Coy Boxing at 5pm at 11am. "C" Coy worked all day on Camp. 1 O/R "A" Coy on leave	96
	17th		Lt. McRae and C.S.M. Nolan from Musketry Course MATRINGHEN. 6 O O/R joined. 1 O/R "B" Coy 1 O/R "C" Coy on leave.	96
	18th		Lt Ross to Hospital. Bn visited by Lieut Lt Col. R.A.M.C. re malaria. 1 O/R "C" Coy and 1 O/R "A" Coy on leave.	96
	19th		Raining during morning. 10 Y am "A" Coy to AUDRESSELLES to erect B.F. tower. A.G. visited and saw men of "Bn" Hedges. Daily guidance parade for everyone commenced. 1 O/R "B" Coy 1 O/R "C" Coy on leave	96
	20th		"A" Coy again went to work at B.F course. B,S,C Coys working and training as usual. 1 O/R "B" Coy on leave	96
	21st		"B" Coy rejoined and re-occupied old billets. "A" and "B" Coys as usual. 1 O/R "C" Coy on leave	96

Army Form C. 2118.

WAR DIARY
—or—
INTELLIGENCE SUMMARY.

(Erase heading not required.) Page 4. #18 (S) BATTALION ROYAL IRISH REGIMENT (PIONEERS)

Place	Date	Hour	Summary of Events and Information	Remarks and references to Appendices
FRANCE	June 1918			
	22"		C.O. inspected billets at 9.30 a.m. Drums accompanied 'B' company on route march at 9 a.m. A. & C. Coys training as usual. 3 O/R 'A' Coy 3 O/R 'B' Coy on leave.	
	23"		Strength Return for week ending Saturday 22nd June 1918. Effective 31 O 733 OR. Admitted to Hospital 21 O/R. Ration 33 O 946 OR. Rejoined from Hospital 23 O/R. Holiday R.C. Service in Church at 10 a.m. C of E Service at 10.30 a.m. in field. Transport Competition in afternoon. 1 O/R 'B' Coy on leave.	
	24"		Coys carried on as usual training. Raining during afternoon. 1 O/R 'A' 1 O/R C Coy on leave.	
	25"		Coys carried on training as usual. Lt. Bailey to Hospital. 1 O/R 'A' 1 O/R 'B' Coy on leave.	
	26"		Holiday for Bn. Sports. Lt. McCarthy-Barry to Hospital. 1 O/R 'A' 1 O/R 'C' Coy on leave.	
	27"		Training as usual. Lt Torrington on leave. Capt. Fraser to Hosp. R.S.M. Daly to Hospital. Lap. Beard from leave. 4 O/R 'A' Coy on leave.	
	28"		Coys training as usual. Cricket match at WISSANT B. Coy winning by one run.	

WAR DIARY
INTELLIGENCE SUMMARY.

Army Form C. 2118.

6th (S) BATTALION ROYAL IRISH REGIMENT (PIONEERS)

Page 5

Place	Date	Hour	Summary of Events and Information	Remarks and references to Appendices
FRANCE	June 1918			
	29th		C.O. inspected billets and kits of 'C' Coy. Capt. Foley joined H.Q. as 2nd in command. C.S.M. Brady joined H.Q. as A/R.S.M. 5 O/R. 6 Coy on leave. Strength Return for week ending Saturday 29th June 1918. Effective 28 O 406 O.R. Admitted to hospital 31 O/R. Ration 30 O 419 O.R. Rejoined from hospital 12 O/R	J.G.
	30th		Holiday. R.C. Service at 10 a.m. Teams played A & B Coys. v. Church. 6 of C. Service at 10.30 a.m. Benediction for R.C.'s at 5.15 p.m. Football match Bn team v machine gun Infantry. 6 O/R 'C' Coy 1 O/R 'B' Coy on leave.	J.G.

Army Form C. 2118.

WAR DIARY
or
INTELLIGENCE SUMMARY.

(Erase heading not required.)

Instructions regarding War Diaries and Intelligence Summaries are contained in F. S. Regs., Part II. and the Staff Manual respectively. Title pages will be prepared in manuscript.

6th (S) BATTALION ROYAL IRISH REGIMENT (PIONEERS)

Effective state of Bn for ten 30 June 1916 B9 & 6

Place	Date	Hour	Summary of Events and Information				Remarks and references to Appendices
			Appointment	Rank	Name	Unit	
(In case of attached officers)			Medical Officer	Captain	HAWKES G.W. M.C.	R.A.M.C.	Present Store
					MITCHELL J.M.		O OR
			R.C. Chaplain Dept	Rev Father	OFARRELL P.	C F 4th Class	28 906 Effective
			2nd in Command	Captain	FOLEY G.R.E.		Attached on Estab. 2
		Kemdy A		"	DAVIS J.C.		Attached for Rations 12
		"			HINTON W.P.		
		"			BEARD E.C. M.C.		
		" B			HENDRY W		Total 30 919
Manchester Regt				Lieut	JONES A.I.W.		
					BRERETON F.S.		3n Detached
					McCRAE T.A.N.		
					BRODERICK W.F.		Riding horses 10
					KING F.J.		Draught horses 55 8
					NORTH H.L.		
					ROCHE M.L.		Pack horses 12
					MALCOMSON A.		Lewis Guns 12
					LOWE A.		
					GODFREY P.J.		Pack Saddlery (set) 12
				2nd Lieut	HUNTER V		G.S. Wagons 6
			Asst Adjutant		EGAN T.J.		G.S. Limbers 4
					HEALY E		
		Transport			McNALLY F.J.		Field Kitchens 3
Roy Munster Fus					BELL W.J.		Water Carts 2
					McAUSLAND J		Maltese cart 1
					WYLIE J		Mess cart 1
Roy Ir Rifles		Offg MO			CLARE J		Bicycles 10
					MEEHAN J.S.		
					DEVANY F.H.		
					STOER E.M.		
		Adjutant		Captain	CUNNINGHAM H.U.		

Original

— CONFIDENTIAL —

WAR DIARY
of
5ᵗʰ Bn Royal Irish Regt (Pioneers)

From 1ˢᵗ July 1918 to 31ˢᵗ July 1918

(Volume 37)

Army Form C. 2118.

WAR DIARY
—or—
INTELLIGENCE SUMMARY.
(Erase heading not required.) PAGE 1

5th (S) BATTALION ROYAL IRISH REGIMENT (PIONEERS)

Instructions regarding War Diaries and Intelligence Summaries are contained in F. S. Regs., Part II. and the Staff Manual respectively. Title pages will be prepared in manuscript.

Place	Date	Hour	Summary of Events and Information	Remarks and references to Appendices
FRANCE	JULY 1918			
	1st		Companies training as usual. Battalion located at TARDINGHEN about 18 kilos from BOULOGNE. 4 O/Ranks 'A' Coy 2 O/Ranks 'B' Coy on leave to U.K. Quinine taken by all ranks.	J.C.
	2nd		Companies training as usual. A.S.C. from WISSANT gave concert in village for Battalion at 6 p.m. 6 O/Ranks 'B' Coy on leave to U.K. Quinine taken by all ranks.	J.C.
	3rd		Companies training as usual in morning. Semi finals of Football at 2.15 p.m. Lt. T.A.N. Mc Rae on leave to U.K. Major R.J. Rees-Mogg D.S.O. joined Bn. 5 O/Ranks 'C' Coy on leave to U.K. Quinine taken by all ranks.	J.C.
	4th		'B' Coy had a Field Day. 'A' and 'C' Coys training as usual. Quinine taken by all ranks. 2 O/Ranks 'A' Coy 2 O/Ranks 'B' Coy 1 O/Rank 'C' Coy on leave.	J.C.
	5th		'A' Coy had a Field Day. "B" and "C" Coys training as usual. Quinine taken by all ranks. 3 O/Ranks 'A' Coy 2 O/Ranks 'B' Coy on leave. Major R.J. Rees-Mogg D.S.O. joined 'A' Coy.	J.C.
	6th		Training as usual during morning hours. Final of Football league in afternoon. Signallers winning. Rev. Father B. O'Farrell M.C. terminated contract and proceeded to U.K. Quinine taken by all ranks. 5 O/R 'B' Coy on leave. Strength Return for week ending Saturday 6th July 1918. Effective 28 0 689 OR Admitted to Hospital 11 O/R Ration 29 0 700 OR Rejoined from Hospital 14 O/R	J.C.

Army Form C. 2118.

WAR DIARY
or
INTELLIGENCE SUMMARY.

(Erase heading not required.) PAGE 2 5th (S) BATTALION ROYAL IRISH REGIMENT (PIONEERS)

Instructions regarding War Diaries and Intelligence Summaries are contained in F. S. Regs., Part II. and the Staff Manual respectively. Title pages will be prepared in manuscript.

Place	Date	Hour	Summary of Events and Information	Remarks and references to Appendices
FRANCE	JULY 1918			
	7/15		Holiday. C of E Service at 9.45 a.m in field. R.C. Service in Chapel by French Priest at 10 a.m. 3pm Bn team played Reserve Vehicle Park WISSANT team winning 2-1. Major G W Hawkes M.C and Lieut W.F Broderick on leave to U.K Major R.J. Rees Mogg D.S.O took command of Battalion. 3 O/R "b" boy on leave. Quinine taken by all ranks.	J.C.
	8		Boys training as usual. Comdg Offr. inspected kits and billets of "C" boy at 11 a.m. Quinine taken by all ranks. 4 O/R "B" boy 1 O/R "C" boy 1 O/R "A" boy on leave	J.C.
	9		Bn. parade at 8 a.m on "C" boys parade ground "A" and "B" boys had field Operations after. Lieut W B. Beutlie from Hospital. Draft of 29 O/Ranks from "L" Infantry Base Depot. Quinine taken by all ranks 4 O/R "A" boy 2 O/R "B" boy on leave	J.C.
	10		"A" and "B" boys training "C" boy had field operations during morning. Bn team played N°12 Bn. Depot at Minerieux at 2.30 p.m resulting in a draw. Slight rain about 10 a.m and again during afternoon. Quinine taken by all ranks. 6 O/Ranks "B" boy on leave	J.C.
	11th		"A" boy had a route march accompanied by Drums. "B" and "C" boys training as usual. Quinine taken by all ranks 2 O/Rank "C" boy on leave	J.C.

Army Form C. 2118.

WAR DIARY
or
INTELLIGENCE SUMMARY.

(Erase heading not required.) PAGE 3 5th (S) BATTALION ROYAL IRISH REGIMENT (PIONEERS)

Place	Date	Hour	Summary of Events and Information	Remarks and references to Appendices
FRANCE	JULY 1918			
	12th		Lieut. M.L. Roche proceeded on leave. Lieut. E. Errington returned from leave. Parade cancelled owing to heavy rain during morning. Quinine taken by all ranks. 2 O/R "B" Coy, 1 O/R "A" Coy and 1 O/R A.S.C. attached on leave.	
	13		Batln (less "B" Coy and Coy Transport) marched from TARDINGHEN at 2 p.m. to entrain at TURLINGTON arriving about 6.30 p.m. 2 lorries conveyed surplus baggage at 3 p.m. Teas issued on arrival of Bn at Station. Transport moved off independently at 1.30 p.m. Train moved out at 10 p.m. Quinine issued to all ranks on station. 3 O/R "B" 2 O/R "A" Coy on leave. Strength Return for week ending Saturday 13th July 1918. Effective 27 O 415 OR. Admitted to Hospital 21 O/R. Ration 28 O 425 OR. Rejoined from Hospital 14 O/R.	
	14th		On train all night and arrived at ARQUES LA BATAILLE about 2 p.m. and marched to No 3 camp MARTIN EGLISE. One lorry conveyed baggage. "C" Company provided loading and unloading party for Bn transport. Raining all morning and afternoon. Quinine issued to all ranks on arrival in camp. 50/R "B" Coy on leave. Batln taken on strength of 50th Division.	

Army Form C. 2118.

WAR DIARY
or
INTELLIGENCE SUMMARY.

(Erase heading not required.) PAGE 4 5th (S) BATTALION ROYAL IRISH REGIMENT (PIONEERS)

Place	Date	Hour	Summary of Events and Information	Remarks and references to Appendices
FRANCE	JULY 1916			
	15"		Boys had rifle inspection and quinine parade in morning. At 1 p.m 'C' Company took over work on Camp Road. At 3 p.m moved to No 1 Camp. Raining slightly from 5 p.m and during night. 6 O/R 'C' Coy on leave.	JG
	16"		Lieut J. Wylie on leave. Boys working on Camp Road. G.O.C inspected the Battn about 10.30 a.m giving only 1/2 hours warning. Carpenters working in Camp erecting cook shelters &c. Coy rifle inspection at 8 a.m daily Quinine issued during afternoon. 4 'B' Coy 1 'A' Coy 1 A S C attached on leave	JG
	17"		Boys started W' work, digging to make tents bomb proof. Carpenters continued with work. 'B' team played 2" Dublin Fusiliers in afternoon winning 2-0. Lieut Baillie superintending work of F.P. Prisoners in quarry. Quinine issued 3 O/R 'A' and 2 O/R 'B' Coy on leave.	JG
	18"		Raining and thunder during forenoon. Boys working on road and preparing sites for tents. Carpenters working as usual. 'B' Coy rejoined, arriving at ARQUES LA BATAILLE at 5.15 p.m Drums played them from station. Teas awaited them on arrival. Quinine issued to all ranks 5 O/R 'B' Coy on leave	JG

Army Form C. 2118.

WAR DIARY
or
INTELLIGENCE SUMMARY.

(Erase heading not required.) PAGE 5 5th (S) BATTALION ROYAL IRISH REGIMENT

Place	Date	Hour	Summary of Events and Information	Remarks and references to Appendices
FRANCE	JULY 1916			
	19th		Carried on with work as usual. Half "B" Coy preparing sites for Officers Tents. Sic Linders drawing gravel from beach at DIEPPE. Quinine issued to all ranks. 5 O/Ranks "C" Coy on leave.	
	20		Lieut J McCausland on leave. Lieut E A McRae from leave. All work carried on as usual. Raining all afternoon. Quinine issued to all ranks. 4 O/Ranks "B" Coy 1 O/Rank "A" Coy on leave. Effective Strength 25 O 404 O.R. Admitted to Hospital 10 O/R Ration Strength 26 O 411 O/R Rejoined from Hospital 4 O/R Return for week Ending Saturday 20 July 1916	
	21st		Holiday. R.C. Service in MARTIN EGLISE CHURCH at 7.30 am Parade at 7 am under 2/Lt Egan. E.J. drums attending. C of E. Service at 10 a.m under Capt A.I.W. Jones. Bn team played 2" Roy. al Munster Fusiliers at 2.30 p.m winning 3 - 1. Quinine taken by all ranks. 6 O/Ranks "C" Coy on leave	
	22		Coys carried on work as usual. 4 G.S wagons drawing chalk from quarry to road. Band of Durham Light Infantry played in Camp during afternoon. Quinine issued to all ranks. 4 O/Ranks "B" Coy. 1 O/R "A" Coy on leave.	

WAR DIARY
or
INTELLIGENCE SUMMARY

(Erase heading not required.) PAGE 6 5th (S) BATTALION ROYAL IRISH REGIMENT (PIONEERS)

Army Form C. 2118.

Place	Date	Hour	Summary of Events and Information	Remarks and references to Appendices
FRANCE	JULY 1918			
	23		Work greatly hindered during day owing to continuous rain. 4 Limbers drawing gravel from beach at DIEPPE. Quinine issued to all ranks. 6 O/Ranks "B" Coy on Leave	✓
	24		Work continued as usual. Occasional showers during day. Quinine issued to all ranks. 4 O/R "C" Coy 1 O/R "A" on Leave	✓
	25		Lieut W. J. Bell on leave. Coys working as usual. Heavy rain during day. Quinine issued to all ranks. 4 O/R "B" Coy on Leave.	✓
	26		Bn Parade at 8 am daily; work continued immediately after. Lieut S.E. Joseph and 33 O/Ranks rejoined from Hospital. Quinine issued to all ranks. Capt J. McAdam field R.A.M.C joined for duty. 2 O/R "C" Coy 3 O/R "B" Coy on Leave.	✓
	27		Work carried on as usual. Occasional showers during day. Band of Durham Light Infantry played in Camp during afternoon. Quinine issued to all ranks. 5 O/Ranks "B" Coy on Leave	✓
			Strength Return for week ending Saturday 27th July 1918 Effective Strength 26 O 449 OR Admitted to Hospital 10 O/R Ration Strength 27 O 459 OR Rejoined from Hospital 5 O/R	✓

WAR DIARY
or
INTELLIGENCE SUMMARY.

Army Form C. 2118.

(Erase heading not required.) PAGE 1   5th (S) BATTALION ROYAL IRISH REGIMENT (PIONEERS)

Place	Date	Hour	Summary of Events and Information	Remarks and references to Appendices
FRANCE	JULY 1918			
	28		Holiday. R.C. Service in MARTIN EGLISE Church at 7.45 a.m. Parade under Lieut. P. J. Godfrey. C of E Service and Presbyterian Service at camp of 13th Black Watch (Scottish Horse) at 9.30 a.m. Leave increased to 10 vacancies per day. Captain J. M. Mitchell R.A.M.C. to 49' Division. Quinine issued to all ranks. 5 O/Rank "B" Coy on Leave	Jo.
	29th		Lieut. M. L. Roche returned off leave. Coys carrying on work as usual. Lieut F. J. King with party of 16 Coy commenced work on laying light railway track from chalk quarry East of Camp to camp road. Quinine issued to all ranks. 4 O/R "B" Coy 2 O/R "C" Coy on Leave	Jo.
	30"		Captain H M Cunningham and 2/Lieut L Healy on leave. Coys working as on 29/15. Quinine issued to all ranks. 6 O/R "B" Coy 2 O/R "C" Coy on Leave	Jo.
	31st		Coys working as usual. Quinine issued to all ranks. 6 O/Ranks "A" Coy 2 O/Rank "B" Coy on Leave	Jo.

H. J. Logan

WAR DIARY
or
INTELLIGENCE SUMMARY

Army Form C. 2118.

(Erase heading not required.)

Nominal State of Before January

PAGE 6 6th (S) BATTALION ROYAL IRISH REGIMENT (PIONEERS)

Place	Date	Hour	Rank	NAME		Summary of Events and Information			Present State		Remarks and references to Appendices
							Rank	NAME			
UNIT			A/C.O. Major	REES-MOGG DSO	R.J.				Effective	O 25	OR 128
In case of attached units			2nd in Command	FOLEY	CRE.	Medical Officer	Captain	HILL	J.McA.		Attached on Estab. 1
			Capt.	HINTON	WR				R.A.M.C.	Attached for Rations	1
				DAVIS	C.J.						7
				BEARD M.C.	EC				Total	26 136	
				HENDRY	W						
				JONES	AM				Riding Horses	Bn.	Attached
			Lieut.	JOSEPH	SG				Draught Horses	10	
Manchester Regt				BRERETON	FS				Pack Horses	47	
				ERRINGTON	E				Lewis Guns	12	
				BAILLIE	WB				Pack Saddlery (sets)	12	
				McRAE	T.A.N.				G.S. Wagons	12	
				NORTH	H.L.				G.S. Limbers	6	
				KING	F.J.				Field Kitchens	7	
				ROCHE	M.L.				Water Carts	3	
				MALCOLMSON	A				Maltese Cart	2	
				LOWE	A				Mess Cart	1	
				GODFREY	P.J.				Bicycles	1	
			2/Lieut	HUNTER	V					9	
				McNALLY	F.J.						
				EGAN	T.J.						
Asst. Adjt.				CLARE	J						
Royal Munster Fus			A/Q.M.	MEEHAN	J.S.						
				DEVANEY	F.H.						
				STOER	M						

Original

CONFIDENTIAL

WAR DIARY

of

5:5 Bn Royal Irish Regt (Pioneers)

from 1st August 1918 to 31st August 1918

Volume 38

WAR DIARY

6th (S) BATTALION ROYAL IRISH REGIMENT (PIONEERS)

INTELLIGENCE SUMMARY

(Erase heading not required.) PAGE 1

Place	Date	Hour	Summary of Events and Information	Remarks and references to Appendices
FRANCE	AUGUST 1918			
	1st		Battalion Parade at 8 a.m. "B" & "D" Coys and "A" Company filling small Box Respirators under Gas Officer. Fatigue boys carried on work on road and camp. Occasional showers during afternoon.	Nil
	2nd		Work greatly hindered by incessant rain during morning and afternoon. Major G.W. Hawkes M.C. rejoined from leave and took over command of the Battalion.	Nil
	3rd		On Parade at 8 am but dismissed at 8.15 am owing to heavy rain which continued throughout the day making further work impossible. Strength return for week ending Saturday 3rd August 1918. Effective 24 O 708 OR Admitted to Hospital 7 OR Ration 25 O 709 OR Rejoined from Hospital 22 OR	Nil
	4th		Holiday. R.C. Service in Church ARQUES - LA - BATAILLE at 9.15 a.m. Parade at 8.15 a.m. under Lieut. P. Godfrey and Lieut. F.H. Devany. C of E Service followed by communion in camp at 8 a.m. C of E Service in camp at 11 am to celebrate 4th Anniversary of the War. Band of 9th Loyal North Lancs played during service. Major G.R.E. Foley and Lieut L.J. Joseph on leave.	Nil

WAR DIARY

Form C. 2118.

5th (S) BATTALION ROYAL IRISH REGIMENT (PIONEERS)

INTELLIGENCE SUMMARY.

(Erase heading not required.) Page 2

Place	Date	Hour	Summary of Events and Information	Remarks and references to Appendices
FRANCE	AUGUST 1918			
	5		8am to 9am Drawing lint bands. 30 yards range allotted to "A" Company for the day. Baths allotted to Bn from 8am to 3.30 pm. Comdg Offr, 2nd in Command, Company Commanders and Adjutant on reconnaissance during afternoon for proposed Tactical Exercise. Raining during afternoon	NIL
	6		"B" Company started work on a new camping ground N.W. of MARTIN EGLISE as it may be necessary to vacate present camp in near future. Had dinners on work returning at 4 pm. "A" Company working on camp. Good and "C" Company on range. Occasional showers during day	NIL
	7		"B" Company went to work on new camp as yesterday but about 2pm work was cancelled. Lieut Hodges on range. "A" Coy worked on road. "C" Company worked on camp	NIL
	8		Bn Inspection Parade at 8 am. "B" Coy working in camp. "B" Coy allotted range for day. "A" Coy working on road. "C" Coy working in camp. Lieut A Lowe on leave. Lieut L.P. McCarthy Barry rejoined from Hospital. Lieut J. Wylie and Lieut J. McDowland from leave	NIL

Army Form C. 2118.

Instructions regarding War Diaries and Intelligence
Summaries are contained in F. S. Regs., Part II.
and the Staff Manual respectively. Title pages
will be prepared in manuscript.

WAR DIARY 5th (S) BATTALION ROYAL IRISH REGIMENT (PIONEERS)
INTELLIGENCE SUMMARY.
(Erase heading not required.) Page 3

Place	Date	Hour	Summary of Events and Information	Remarks and references to Appendices
FRANCE	AUGUST 1918			
	9th		An Inspection Parade 8am. Range allotted to "C" Company for day	
			"A" Company working on road. "B" Coy working on camp. Commanding	
			Officer and Company Commanders again reconnoitred ground for Divisional	
			Tactical Exercise	Nil
	10th		Divisional Tactical Exercise in which "Bn took part. Parade in fighting	
			Order with Steel Helmets at 8.30 am. Marched off 8.50 am to pass starting	
			Point at 9 am en route to COQUEREAUMONT the A.P. arriving there at 10 am	
			On orders being received from C.R.E. the companies moved off to work as	
			follows :- "A" Coy clearing road in Right Brigade front. "B" Company in Left	
			Brigade front. "C" Coy clearing ANCOURT of debris etc. 2nd Lieut Hodgson & Church	
ANCOURT			Returned to Camp at 1.45 p.m. Lieut E.J McNally on leave	
			Lieut J.D Meehan taking over transport	
			Strength. Return for week ending Saturday 10th August 1918	
			Effective 26 O 710 O.R Admitted to Hospital 2 O.R	
			Ration 27 O 711 O.R Rejoined from Hospital 36 O.R	Nil
	11th		Holiday R.C Service in Church MARTIN EGLISE at 8:30 am. Parade at 8am under Lt Pvt L. Roche	
			and D.C Olsen. C of E Service in camp at 10.45 am Lt W. B Baillie taking	

WAR DIARY

INTELLIGENCE SUMMARY

(Erase heading not required.) Page 4

Place	Date	Hour	Summary of Events and Information	Remarks and references to Appendices
FRANCE	AUGUST 1918			
	11th (contd)		Change of parade. Church of England Service in Y.M.C.A. at 9.30 am. Draft W.O. Bell from leave.	nil
	12"	9am to 11 am.	"B" and "C" Coys and 1/2 Regimental Transport at Divisional Gas Test from 2am to 4am. "A" Coy Hdqrs and remainder Transport from 9am to 11am. 2nd in command and Quarter "A" Coy allotted range up to mid-day. "A" Coy Master attended lecture on "Supplies in the Field" at Divisional Train. Lieut. J. McAusland transferred to 15th Royal Irish Rifles.	nil
	13		Baths allotted to "Batln" from 8am to 3.30pm. "B" Coy working on road up to mid-day. "A" Coy then taking over work for afternoon party of "D" Company firing on range. "B" Company Bombing under Bombing Off. 10 Officers attending lectures at Div. Gas Test for a period 13" to 18" inst. "B" Coy digging trenches N.E. of MARTIN EGLISE. A.S.C. Coys less 1 Platoon working on road. "B" Company working on transport Lines. 1 section "B" Coy Bombing. Hd Qrs allotted range for day. All Officers attended a lecture on Aeroplanes in the School House MARTIN EGLISE at 5.30 pm.	nil
	14			nil

Army Form C. 2118.

WAR DIARY

5th (S) BATTALION ROYAL IRISH REGIMENT (PIONEERS)

INTELLIGENCE SUMMARY

(Erase heading not required.) Page 5

Instructions regarding War Diaries and Intelligence Summaries are contained in F. S. Regs., Part II. and the Staff Manual respectively. Title pages will be prepared in manuscript.

Place	Date	Hour	Summary of Events and Information	Remarks and references to Appendices
FRANCE 1918				
	AUGUST. 15"		"C" Coy & 1 Platoon digging trenches as "B" Company were previous day. 2 Platoons "B" Company working on Transport Lines and 2 Platoons on Range. 1 Platoon "B" Coy on Camp Quarry and 1 Section "C" Company bombing. "A" Company on road. 4 Limbers drawing gravel from DIEPPE	Nil
	16"		"A" Company on Louis Road. "B" Company on Quarry. MARTIN EGLISE relieving "C" Camp for dinners. "C" Coy digging trenches as yesterday with one Platoon on Camp Quarry. "B" & "D" as on range	Nil
	17"		"A" and "B" boys as yesterday. 2 Platoons "B" Coy on range, one Platoon on Transport Lines and one Platoon closing tent sites in new camp. Captain W. Cunningham and Lieut. E. Healy from leave. Lieut. Brereton on leave. Strength Return for week ending Saturday 17" August { Effective 24 O 754 OR Admitted 16 Hospital 2 OR Ration 25 O 752 OR Discharged from Hospital 36 OR	Nil
	18"		Holiday. R.C. Service at 8.15 am in Church MARTIN EGLISE under Lieut E. Healy. C of E at 8 am in Camp under Lieut J. A. McRae. Presbyterian in Y.M.C.A. tent at 9.45 am. Divisional Horse Show at DIEPPE	Nil

Army Form C. 2118.

WAR DIARY
5th BATTALION ROYAL IRISH REGIMENT (PIONEERS)

INTELLIGENCE SUMMARY
(Erase heading not required.) PAGE 6

Instructions regarding War Diaries and Intelligence Summaries are contained in F. S. Regs., Part II. and the Staff Manual respectively. Title pages will be prepared in manuscript.

Place	Date	Hour	Summary of Events and Information	Remarks and references to Appendices
FRANCE	AUGUST			
	19		On Parade at 8am. "A" Coy working on road and "B" Coy in quarry. One Platoon "C" Coy working on Transport Lines and remainder training in rapid wiring and bombing	Nil
	20		"A" Coy working on road and "B" Coy in quarry. 1 Platoon "C" Coy on Transport Lines remainder rapid wiring and using 30 yards range	Nil
	21		On Parade at 8am. "A" and "B" Coys working as previous day. One Platoon "C" Coy on Transport Lines remainder on ranges and bombing. Lieut. L. S. Joseph rejoined from leave	Nil
	22		Lewis Gunners of "A" and "B" Coys on ranges morning. Coys carried on work on road and Transport Lines. Lieut W. B. Baillie on leave	Nil
	23		On Parade at 8am. 2 N.C.O's of each Coy commenced four days bombing course under Lieut Devany. "A" Company working in quarry. "B" Coy on road. One Platoon "C" Coy on Transport Lines, remainder "C" Coy training. Lt Malcomson on leave	Nil

Army Form C. 2118.

WAR DIARY
INTELLIGENCE SUMMARY.
(Erase heading not required.) PAGE 7

(S) BATTALION ROYAL IRISH REGIMENT (PIONEERS)

Instructions regarding War Diaries and Intelligence Summaries are contained in F. S. Regs., Part II. and the Staff Manual respectively. Title pages will be prepared in manuscript.

Place	Date	Hour	Summary of Events and Information	Remarks and references to Appendices
FRANCE	AUGUST 1918			
	24		"A" and "B" Coys working as usual. Two Sections "C" Coy on range remainder refund wiring. All men with revolvers on range. Conferance heard from 5-7 p.m.	NIL
			Strength Return for Week ending Saturday 24th August 1918	
			Effective 25 O 706 OR Admitted to Hospital 1 O O.R.	
			Ration 26 O 707 OR Discharged from Hospl. 17 O.R.	
	25		Holiday. R.C. Service in MARTIN EGLISE Church at 10.30 am under Lieut North. Holy Communion C of E Service in Camp at 8.30 am under Lieut North. Holy Communion at 9 am. Non-conformist Service at 9.45 am in Y.M.C.A. Tent MARTIN EGLISE.	NIL
	26		'A' & 'B' Coys proceeded with work on road. 'C' Coy training and using range. Lieut O'd McNally rejoined from leave.	NIL
	27		Tactical scheme held by C.R.E. in which Bn took part. Left camp at 7.45 am in fighting order and marched to rendez vous where verbal orders were issued by C.R.E. for the construction of a line of defences by Field Coys R.E. and Pioneers to be occupied by a retreating Division. Bn. returned to camp when trenches had been marked out. At 5.30 p.m. C.R.E. held conference of all Pioneer Officers en Officers Mess regarding the work of the day. Lieut. V. Hamlin on leave	NIL

A6945 Wt. W11422/M1160 350,000 12/16 D. D. & L. Forms/C/2118/14.

WAR DIARY
INTELLIGENCE SUMMARY.

Army Form C. 2118.

(3/5) BATTALION ROYAL IRISH REGIMENT

Page 8

Place	Date	Hour	Summary of Events and Information	Remarks and references to Appendices
FRANCE	AUGUST 1918			
	28		"A" and "B" Coys working as usual. 1 Platoon "C" Coy on Transport Lines	Nil
			Remainder bombing and rapid wiring	
	29		"A" Coy working on road and "B" Coy in quarry. 1 Platoon "C" Coy on	Nil
			Transport Lines. Remainder on range. Lieut. F.J. King on leave	
	30		"A" & "B" Coys working as usual. One Platoon "C" Coy on Transport Lines	Nil
			Rain interrupted work all day. Lieut. S. Godfrey on leave	
	31		"D" Coy working on road and "B" Coy on quarry. 1 Platoon "C" Coy	
			on Transport Lines and remainder training in gas and bombing	
			10 grains of quinine were taken every day during the month by all	
			ranks	
			Strength return for week ending Saturday 31st August 1918 Admitted to Hospital 13 OR	Nil
			Effective 22 O 594 OR	
			Ration 23 O 594 OR Rejoined from Hospital 11 OR	

M. Cunningham Capt.

Army Form C. 2118.

WAR DIARY
or
INTELLIGENCE SUMMARY.

5th (8) BATTALION ROYAL IRISH REGIMENT (PIONEERS)

(Erase heading not required.)

Instructions regarding War Diaries and Intelligence Summaries are contained in F. S. Regs., Part II. and the Staff Manual respectively. Title pages will be prepared in manuscript.

Place	Date	Hour	Summary of Events and Information				Remarks and references to Appendices
			Appoint	Rank	Name		
UNIT			Medical Officer	Captain	HILL J.M.F.A	R.A.M.C	
In case of Officer attached							
			Present State				
			Effective				O.R. 594
			Attached on Estab.				22
			Attached for Rations				1
			Total				23 594
			Riding Horses				9
			Draught Horses				38
			Mules				17
			Pack Horses				4
			Mules				8
			Lewis Guns				12
			Pack Saddlery (sets)				12
			G.S. Wagons				6
			G.S. Limbers				4
			Field Kitchens				3
			Water Carts				2
			Maltese Carts				1
			Travs Cart				1
			Bicycles				9

			Appoint	Rank	Name		
Manchester Regt			C.O.	Lt Col	HAWKES G.W. M.C.		
			2nd i/c	Major	REES-MOGG R.J. D.S.O		
				Capt	HINTON W.P.		
					BEARD E.C. M.C.		
					HENDRY W.		
					JONES A.I.W.		
					DAVIS C.J.		
			Adjt.	Capt	CUNNINGHAM H.U.		
				Lieut	JOSEPH S.G.		
					ERRINGTON E.		
					McCARTHY-BARRY R.L.		
					NORTH H.L.		
					McRAE T.A.N.		
					ROCHE M.L.		
				2/Lieut	GREER E.		
Roy Munster Fus			Tpt. Offr.		McNALLY F.J.		
Roy Irish Rifles					HEALY E.		
					WYLIE J.		
					BELL W.J.		
					MEEHAN J.S.		
					DEVANY F.H.		
					STOER E.M.		

Original

CONFIDENTIAL

WAR DIARY
of
5ᵗʰ Bn ROYAL IRISH REGIMENT (Pioneers)

from 1ˢᵗ September 1918 to 30ᵗʰ September 1918

VOLUME 39

Army Form C. 2118.

WAR DIARY
INTELLIGENCE SUMMARY. 6th (S) BATTALION ROYAL IRISH REGIMENT (PIONEER)
(Erase heading not required.) PAGE 1.

Instructions regarding War Diaries and Intelligence Summaries are contained in F. S. Regs., Part II. and the Staff Manual respectively. Title pages will be prepared in manuscript.

Place	Date	Hour	Summary of Events and Information	Remarks and references to Appendices
FRANCE	SEPTEMBER 1918			
	1st		Holiday. R.C. service at 9 a.m in Moralin Eglise Church under 2 Lieut Skeen C of E service in bank at 8.30 a.m under Lieut Greer followed by Holy Communion at 9 a.m. Non-conformist service in Y.M.C.A Moralin Eglise at 10 a.m.	xxx
	2nd		On Parade at 8 a.m. "A" Coy trench digging and musketry according to plans by C.R.E. 50th Div. in morning and practising musketry in afternoon. "B" Coy firing on 200 and 300 yards range having dinner out. 2 Platoons "C" Coy working on road. 1 Platoon in quarry and 1 Platoon rapid wiring	xxx
	3rd		On Inspection Parade at 8 a.m "A" Coy continued in trenches as on previous day. "B" Coy using long range. 3 Platoon "C" Coy on road and 1 Platoon rapid wiring. Capt. A.S.W. Jones to England for duty with R.A.F.	xxx
	4th		A route march held under Divisional arrangements in which Bn took part. Parade at 9.15 a.m full marching order pack wearing steel helmets and carrying box respirators in alert position. Moved off to arrive at S.P. before 9.47 a.m when march started. Course of 13½ miles as modified out by 50th Div was followed and 10 minutes rest in every hour was allowed. Bn returned to Lecelle by 2.30 pm and had dinner. Five men fell out owing to foot trouble	xxx

WAR DIARY
INTELLIGENCE SUMMARY.
5th (S) BATTALION ROYAL IRISH REGIMENT (PION.)
PAGE 2

Army Form C. 2118.

Place	Date	Hour	Summary of Events and Information	Remarks and references to Appendices
FRANCE	SEPTEMBER 1918			
	5		"A" Coy using long range. "B" Coys 2 Platoons working for "A" Coy and 2 Platoons musketry in trenches. "C" Coy working on road	[sig]
	6		"A" Coy Bombing. 1 Platoon "B" Coy on road remainder musing. "C" Coy working on road.	[sig]
	7		Coys employed as on previous day. Rain interrupted work. Strength Return for week ending Saturday 7th September 1918. Effective 23 O 657 OR Ration 23 O 657 OR Admitted to Hospital 9 OR Regained from Hospital 23 OR	[sig]
	8		Holiday R.C Service in Marlin Eglise Church at 11 am under Lieut McCarthy. Granny. C of E Service in Camp at 8.50 am under Lieut E Errington Horley. Non conformist service at 10 am in Y.M.C.A. Communion followed. General H.C. Jackson DSO founds 50" Division visited and inspected Camp at noon	*[sig]
	9		"A" Coy on musketry and arm drills in morning. Kit Inspection in afternoon. "B" Coy Rapid wiring and bombing. "C" Coy working on road in morning and had Kit Inspection in afternoon.	[sig]

WAR DIARY
INTELLIGENCE SUMMARY (5) BATTALION ROYAL IRISH REGIMENT (PIONS)

PAGE 3

Army Form C. 2118.

Place	Date	Hour	Summary of Events and Information	Remarks and references to Appendices
FRANCE	SEPTEMBER 1916			
	10th		Bn Parade fell in at 8am but was dismissed on account of heavy rain	
			Work was started on road later but continuous rain cancelled arrangements	✗✗✗
	11th		Holiday in afternoon for Bn Sports which were held at DIEPPE	✗✗✗
			Bn left b/Os parade at 8.30am and afterwards proceeded to work on New Camp Road	
	12th		Bn paraded 6.45 am strong as possible with blank ammunition to take part in Divisional Tactical Operations. Battle Order with Regt. Transport	✗✗✗ ✗✗✗
	13th		Bn proceeded with work on Camp Road	
	14th		A bomb range 300 yards range "B" and "C" Coys working on road	
			Strength Returns for week ending Saturday 14th September 1916	
			Effective 29 O 804 OR Admitted to Hospital 14 OR	✗✗✗
			Ration 30 O 804 OR Rejoined from Hospital 12 OR	✗✗✗
	15th		Bn preparing for a move	
	16th		Moved by rail (less "C" Coy which followed at 4 p.m.) from ROUXMESNIL Station to DOULLENS. Left 12.36. Arrived 10.30 pm and marched about 11.30 pm to WARLINCOURT where billeted	✗✗✗

WAR DIARY
INTELLIGENCE SUMMARY.
(Erase heading not required.) PAGE 4

Army Form C. 2118.

5th (S) BATTALION ROYAL IRISH REGIMENT (PIONEERS)

Place	Date	Hour	Summary of Events and Information	Remarks and references to Appendices
FRANCE	SEPTEMBER 1915			
	17		Arrived WARLINCOURT at 6 a.m. LENS 11 Map Ref. 5 men fell out with malaria during march when heavy rain and thunder storm took place. "C" Coy arrived at 8.30 a.m. No further parades except cleaning up billets	
	18		Coys cleaning billets and parades (silence economy)	
	19		Parades under Coy arrangements. "C" Coy had short route march. Capt W Hunter Lieut Ire Bailey Bonny and Lieut North reported and departed for 2nd Bn Royal Irish Regt. Capt D. L. Joseph took command of "A" Coy. Lieut A. Malcomson took up Signalling Duties	
	20		Parades from 8 till 12, 1.30 till 3.30 under Company arrangements. No 9 Platoon "C" Coy went to LUCHEUX for Final Divisional Shooting Competition winning same by 10 points	
	21st		Parades from 8 till 12, 1.30 till 3.30, marching by compass day & night work	
			Strength Return for Week ending Saturday 21st September 1915.	
			Effective 28 O 831 OR Admitted to Hospital 15 OR	
			Ration 29 O 832 OR Rejoined from Hospital 12 OR	

WAR DIARY
INTELLIGENCE SUMMARY

6th (S) BATTALION ROYAL IRISH REGIMENT (PIONEER)

PAGE 5

Army Form C. 2118.

Place	Date	Hour	Summary of Events and Information	Remarks and references to Appendices
FRANCE	SEPTEMBER 1918			
	22nd		Holiday. Church Parades R.C. 9 a.m. WARLINCOURT Church. Presbyterian at 10.15 a.m. in "B" Coys billet. C of E at 11 a.m. on Parade Ground. Lecture on Tanks by Lt Col. Mecklen D.S.O. M.C. at MONDICOURT. Two Officers and one N.C.O. per Company attended	
	23rd		Parades from 8 till 12 and 1.30 till 3.30 under Company arrangements. 2/Lt Devaney to England for duty with R.A.F.	
	24th		Parades 8 till 12, 1.30 till 3.30. G.O.C. visited billets and gave prizes to No 9 Platoon for winning Divisional Rifle Competition. Warning order received regarding move to MONTIGNY Area.	
	25th		Bn making preparations for move	
	26th		Transport left WARLINCOURT 4.45 a.m. Bn left WARLINCOURT 9.45 a.m. by bus. Bn arrived BEAUCOURT 12.45 p.m. and Transport arrived 2 p.m. Bn billeted in village. HdQrs in Chateau.	
	27th		Orders received for move to COMBLES Area. Transport left at 12.5 and marched to FRICOURT where they bivouacked for the night	

WAR DIARY

INTELLIGENCE SUMMARY. 5th (S) BATTALION ROYAL IRISH REGIMENT (PIONEERS)

PAGE 6

Army Form C. 2118.

Place	Date	Hour	Summary of Events and Information	Remarks and references to Appendices
FRANCE	SEPTEMBER 1918			
	28th		Bn. less Transport, left BEAUCOURT by Bus at 1pm arrived COMBLES	
		6pm	Transport arrived at 5 p.m. Battle surplus left with Bn.	WAA
			9 Officers 20 Other Ranks	
			Strength Return for Week Ending Saturday 28th September 1918	
			Effective 1/28 O 844 OR Admitted to Hospital 8 OR	WAA
			Ration 29 O 845 OR Rejoined from Hospital 8 OR	WAA
	29th		Coys employed entraining Billets	WAA
	30th		Coys employed as on previous day. Warning order received for	WAA
			move to EPEHY area	

Thos A. McRae

WAR DIARY or INTELLIGENCE SUMMARY

Army Form C. 2118.

5th (S) BATTALION ROYAL IRISH REGIMENT (PIONEERS)

Effective State of Bn for 30th September 1916 PAGE 7

Place	Date	Hour	Appoint	Rank	Name		Summary of Events and Information			Remarks and references to Appendices
							Unit	Appointment	Rank	Name	Present State	
UNIT											
In care of attached Officers			C.O.	A/Lt.Col	HAWKES M.C.	G.W.	R.A.M.C.	Medical Officer	Captain	HILL J. MRA	Effective	O. 25 OR 813
			2nd i/c	A/Major	EOLEY	GRE				In 10 days leave to UK 16/6/30	Attached on estab	1
			Captain	Captain	BEARD M.C.	EC	R.A.M.C.	A/M.O. in Charge	"	RIMMER R	Attached for Rations	- -
			"	"	HENDRY	W					Total	26 814
			"	"	DAVIS	C.J.						
			"	"	JOSEPH	S.G.						
			"	Lieut	ERRINGTON	E						
			"	"	KING	F.J.						Attached
			A/Adjt	"	McRAE	TAN						
			"	"	BAILLIE	W.B.						3
			"	"	ROCHE	M.L.					Riding Horses	10
			"	"	MALCOMSON	A						
			"	"	LOWE	A					Draught Horses	57
			"	"	HUNTER	V						
Manchester Regt				2/	GREER	E					Pack Horses	12
Black Watch, TF				"	CARNEGIE	RY						
				"	McNally	F.J.					Lewis Guns	12
Roy. Munster Fus				"	HEALY	E						
Royal Irish Rifles				"	BELL	W.J.					Pack Saddlery (sets)	12
				"	WYLIE	J						
			A/Qr. Mr	"	CLARE	J					G.S. Wagons	9
				"	MULLAN M.C.	P.A.						
				"	MEEHAN	J.S.					G.S. Limbers	7
				"	STOER	F.M.						
				"	HUNTER	HAR					Field Kitchens	3
				"	O'SHEA	J.V.						
				"	RICHARDSON	C.A.					Water Carts	2
			Adjutant	A/Capt	CUNNINGHAM	H.U.						
											Mallise Cart	1
											Mess Cart	1
											Bicycles	9

Original

CONFIDENTIAL

WAR DIARY

of

5ᵗʰ Bn Royal Irish Regt. (Pioneers)

From 1ˢᵗ October 1918 to 31ˢᵗ October 1918

Volume 40

Army Form C. 2118.

WAR DIARY
INTELLIGENCE SUMMARY.
(Erase heading not required.) PAGE 1

Instructions regarding War Diaries and Intelligence
Summaries are contained in F. S. Regs., Part II.
and the Staff Manual respectively. Title pages
will be prepared in manuscript.

Place	Date	Hour	Summary of Events and Information	Remarks and references to Appendices
FRANCE	OCTOBER 1918			
	1st		Battalion including Transport left COMBLES at 1000 hours and marched to EPEHY, about 15 miles. Dress fighting order. Sacks and blankets carried by lorries. Arrived EPEHY 1630 hours. Battn billeted in village in cellars.	
	2nd		"A" Coy worked from LEMPIRE to TOMBOIS FARM repairing road	
			"B" Coy worked on LEMPIRE - VENDHUILE road repairing same	
			"C" Coy worked on LEMPIRE - VENDHUILE road repairing same.	
			No casualties	
	3rd		"B" Company following up Brit attack on LE CATELET making and repairing road from F.30.a.9.9. through BONY to LE CATELET. Work only put through as far as A15.b.1.4 owing to enemy fire and observation. It was completed same night by 444/Coy R.E. Hours of work 0500-1730. Casualties 1killed 1 wounded	
			"C" boy working from A.19.a.12 - A.20.c.05 BONY MT ST MARTIN road A18.d.7.1 making Horse Transport track and clearing and filling shell holes. Was held up owing to enemy fire and observation. Casualties 1 man wounded	
			"A" boy in reserve at EPEHY (improving billets)	

Army Form C. 2118.

WAR DIARY
INTELLIGENCE SUMMARY.
(Erase heading not required.) PAGE 2

Instructions regarding War Diaries and Intelligence Summaries are contained in F. S. Regs., Part II. and the Staff Manual respectively. Title pages will be prepared in manuscript.

Place	Date	Hour	Summary of Events and Information	Remarks and references to Appendices
FRANCE	OCTOBER 1918			
	4		"A" Coy continued work from TOMBOIS FARM towards VENDHUILLE filling shell holes and improving road. No casualties	WM
			"B" Coy working on LEMPIRE - VENDHUILLE Road filling shell holes and improving road. No casualties	WM
			"C" Coy making bridge suitable for carrying horse transport at A12c4.9 with lines cut at side. Also making road from bridge through A12d and B4a to B1a.	WM
	5		"A" Coy working from TOMBOIS FARM towards VENDHUILLE improving and repairing road.	WM
			"B" Coy assisting 283rd A.T. Coy R.E. in erecting INGLIS bridge across ST QUENTIN CANAL	WM
			"C" Coy working on VENDHUILLE road improving and repairing road also making deviation from road to canal bank for tanks for foot bridge. No casualties	WM
			Strength return for week ending Saturday 5th October 1918. Admitted to Hospital 9 O.R. Effective strength 24 O 799 O.R. Rejoined from Hospital —	
			Ration strength 250 802 O.R.	WM

Army Form C. 2118.

WAR DIARY
or
INTELLIGENCE SUMMARY.
(Erase heading not required.) PAGE 3

Instructions regarding War Diaries and Intelligence Summaries are contained in F. S. Regs., Part II. and the Staff Manual respectively. Title pages will be prepared in manuscript.

Place	Date	Hour	Summary of Events and Information	Remarks and references to Appendices
FRANCE	OCTOBER 1918			
	6th		Bath. Hd Qrs moved from EPEHY at 1000 hours and proceeded to QUINNET COPSE. Carried on old trenches. Coys carried Rd Con on completion of days work.	2cwn
			"B" Coy assisting 253rd R.E Coy in erecting INGLIS bridge over ST QUENTIN Canal at VENDHUILE. "A" Coy working on road from GRANDCOURT to LORMISSET - BELLUE FARM - BEAUREVOIR. 4 casualties. 1 man since died of wounds.	2cwn
	7th		"C" Coy making road passable for Motor lorries through VENDHUILLE - LE CATELET - GOUY. "B" Coy. One Platoon assisting 141st Coy RE working on trestle bridge at VENDHUILLE. Remainder of Coy making PUTNEY- PIEANE Road fit for wheel traffic. Work completed.	2cwn
	8th		"A" Coy working on road from GOUY to VAUXHALL QUARRY. "C" Coy Remetalling bridge at A12 c4.2. Improving roads round A 6 c4.2. "A" Coy working on road from LE CATELET to PIENNE. "B" Coy. 1 Platoon at VENDHUILLE BRIDGE 1 Platoon embussing troops from PIEANE to VAUXHALL QUARRY. 2 Platoons billeted repairing. "C" Coy Maintenance of road from PUTNEY- GOUY.	2cwn

Army Form C. 2118.

WAR DIARY
INTELLIGENCE SUMMARY.
(Erase heading not required.) Page 4

Place	Date	Hour	Summary of Events and Information	Remarks and references to Appendices
FRANCE	OCTOBER 1918			
	9"		Coys working as usual. Work cancelled at 1300. Baths cancelled at Gouy and barracked for night. A Coy working on road from Gouy to VILLERS OUTREAUX. B. Coy working on VENDHUILE ROAD to BEAUX Bridge. C. Coy working on Gavril Bridge with R.E. Coy. "C" Coy working on road from GOUY to GOUY, BELLAIN Railway at footer bridge at VENDHUILE.	XXIV
	10.		Bath moved from GOUY to MARETZ starting at 0830. Billeted in town	XXIV
	11		Bath rested in MARETZ. Coys employed cleaning & improving billets and intercommunication.	XXIV
	12		A Coy working on road from MARETZ to BUSIGNY. B. Coy working on road from BUSIGNY to HONNECHY. "C" Coy working on BUSIGNY - LE CATEAU Road. Strength Return for week ending Saturday 12 October 19:18. Effective Strength 23 O 749 OR. Admitted to Hospital 9 OR. Ration Strength 24 O 752 OR. Evacuated from Hospital 1 OR.	XXIV
	13"		C. Coy working on BUSIGNY - LE CATEAU Road improving road and drainage. Including site of pave. A Coy working on MARETZ - BUSIGNY Road. B. Coy working on cross Rds at REUMONT and point where BUSIGNY / LE CATEAU Road crosses REUMONT ST. SOUPLET ROAD.	XXIV

(Ag675) W. W438/P360 600,000 12/17 D. & S. L. **Both Sides**. Forms/C2118/15.

WAR DIARY
or
INTELLIGENCE SUMMARY.
(Erase heading not required.) PAGE 5

Army Form C. 2118.

Instructions regarding War Diaries and Intelligence Summaries are contained in F. S. Regs., Part II. and the Staff Manual respectively. Title pages will be prepared in manuscript.

Place	Date	Hour	Summary of Events and Information	Remarks and references to Appendices
FRANCE	OCTOBER 1918			
	14		C Coy working on BUSIGNY - LE CATEAU ROAD improving track and drainage	72M
			A Coy working on MARETZ - BUSIGNY Road	72M
			B Coy working on roads at REUMONT and at point where BUSIGNY-LE CATEAU Road crosses REUMONT - ST SOUPLET Road	72M
	15		A Coy working on MARETZ - BUSIGNY Road. C Coy working on BUSIGNY - LE CATEAU Road improving track and drainage. B Coy working at roads at REUMONT and at roads where BUSIGNY - LE CATEAU Road crosses REUMONT - ST SOUPLET Road	72M
	16		A Coy rested in billets at MARETZ. 2 Officers &q of Coy repairing bridges with R.E. to throw across River SELLE	72M
			C Coy reported to O.C. 11th Coy R.E. at MOONECHY and proceeded to River 2000 x N.W. of St SOUPLET for work on foot bridges over River SELLE	72M
			B Coy completed cables at REUMONT at point where BUSIGNY LE CATEAU Road crossed REUMONT - ST SOUPLET Road. Reconnaissance of ESCAUFOURT ST BENIN Road by O.C. "B" Coy	72M

Army Form C. 2118.

WAR DIARY
or
INTELLIGENCE SUMMARY.
(Erase heading not required.) PAGE 6

Instructions regarding War Diaries and Intelligence Summaries are contained in F. S. Regs., Part II. and the Staff Manual respectively. Title pages will be prepared in manuscript.

Place	Date	Hour	Summary of Events and Information	Remarks and references to Appendices
OCTOBER	1918			
	12th		"A" Coy & Queens 5th C/Ranks assisting R.E. Knocking Bridge across River SELLE	ZUM
			Remainder of Coy making approach in road around ST BENIN. Heavy shelling in sunken	
			"C" Coy carrying bridge forward to River SELLE and preparing them under	ZUM
			river of barrage punctually to cross if casualties	ZUM
			"B" Coy working on approach in ST BENIN during first attack & 2 casualties	
	13th		"A" Coy worked on road E of St BENIN area ford under Railway Bridge and made	ZUM
			Sunken Track towards BASUEL. Prepared material for and partly erected bridge on SELLE	
			"C" Coy working on FASSIAUX Railway Bridge cleaning and making road fit for	ZUM
			horse transport from Railway Bridge to LE QUENNELET GRANGE	
			"B" Coy 2 Platoons mopping up in LE CATEAU station and 1 working in ST BENIN	
			1 boy billeted in HONNECHY on completion of days work	
			Strength Return for Saturday week ending 12th October 1918	ZUM
			Effectives 26 O 884 OR Admitt sick hospital 23 OR	
			Ration 27 O 830 OR Rejoined from hospitals 15 OR	

WAR DIARY
INTELLIGENCE SUMMARY.
(Erase heading not required.) PAGE 7

Army Form C. 2118.

Instructions regarding War Diaries and Intelligence Summaries are contained in F. S. Regs., Part II. and the Staff Manual respectively. Title pages will be prepared in manuscript.

Place	Date	Hour	Summary of Events and Information	Remarks and references to Appendices
FRANCE	OCTOBER 1918			
	19"		"A" Coy. noted in billets at MARETZ. Interior economy (Baths, cleaning etc.)	
			"C" Coy. noted in billets at MARETZ	
			"B" Coy. noted in billets at HONNECHY. B/Cd. and 2nd i/c "B" Coy. made a reconnaissance for motor road to BASUEL	2am
	20"		"A" Coy. working on road from ST BENIN to LE QUENNELET GRANGE. improving and repairing road. "B" Coy. improving dry weather track from FASSIAUX Bridge to LE QUENNELET FARM. "C" Coy. resting (Interior economy)	2am
	21"		"A" Coy. marched from MARETZ. Worked from LE QUENNELET GRANGE to LE CATEAU improving and repairing road and filling shell holes. Casualties 2 killed and 2 wounded. 1 Prisoner taken in trailing at LE CATEAU STATION. "B" Coy. improving road from LE QUENNELET GRANGE to BASUEL	2am
			"C" Coy. working on part of LE CATEAU-WASSIGNY road & LE CATEAU-MAZINGHIEN Road. Filling shell holes and filling for motor transport	2am
			"A" Coy. working on BUSIGNY-LE CATEAU Road improving and repairing road and filling shell holes. "C" Coy. resting in billets at LE CATEAU. "B" Coy. move to billets near LE CATEAU STATION. Coy. shelled in billets. 3 men killed 23 wounded	2am

WAR DIARY
or
INTELLIGENCE SUMMARY.

(Erase heading not required.) PAGE 8

Army Form C. 2118.

Place	Date	Hour	Summary of Events and Information	Remarks and references to Appendices
FRANCE	OCTOBER 1918			
	23		"A" Coy maintaining roads nr. LE BASUEL. "C" Coy (Wilson) clearing road	XXM
			at PASSIAUX BRIDGE.	
			"B" Coy working by night in 2 shifts on clearing of railway bridge on LE CATEAU -	
			BAZUEL ROAD.	
	24		"A" Coy clearing debris of demolished railway bridge on LE CATEAU - BASUEL Road	XXM
			"B" Coy working in billets at LE CATEAU STATION	
			"C" Coy working at (1) PASSEAUX BRIDGE (2) Road through POMMEREUIL 400' N x 40° S	
			(3) Main Road in LE CATEAU in direction of LANDRECIES clearing and filling shell holes	
			and repairing roads. B. Hedges moved up to MARETZ.	
	25		"A" Coy clearing debris of demolished Railway Bridge on LE CATEAU - BASUEL Road	XXM
			"B" Coy improving LE CATEAU - LE QUENNELET FARM Road	
			"C" Coy working on Road from LE CATEAU to MAZINGHIEN clearing and repairing roadway	
	26		"A" Coy clearing debris of demolished railway bridge on LE CATEAU - BAZUEL Road	XXM
			"B" Coy improving LE CATEAU - QUENNELET FARM Road	
			"C" Coy working on Road from LE CATEAU to MAZINGHIEN and from LE QUENNELET	XXM
			FARM to 400' towards BASUEL clearing road, draining and filling shell holes	

WAR DIARY
INTELLIGENCE SUMMARY.

(Erase heading not required.) PAGE 9

Army Form C. 2118.

Place	Date	Hour	Summary of Events and Information	Remarks and references to Appendices
FRANCE	OCTOBER 1918		Strength Return for Week Ending Saturday 26 October 1916.	
			Effective 24 O 813 OR Admitted to Hospital 35 OR	
			Ration 28 O 814 OR Returned from Hospitals 15 OR	WM
	27		"A" Coy working on LE CATEAU - WASSIGNY Road and road W. side of QUENNELET FARM improving, repairing and drainage	
			"B" Coy 2 platoons working on LE CATEAU - BUSIGNY Road	
			"C" Coy working from LE CATEAU to Road Junction for BASUEL and thence to LE QUENNELET FARM filling shell holes and improving road for Motor Transport traffic, also improving drainage	WM
	28		"A" Coy worked on POMMEREUIL - FONTAINE Road improving and filling shell holes	
			"B" Coy worked on the CATEAU - POMMEREUIL Road and roads in POMMEREUIL Area. "C" Coy working from Road Junction E. of LE CATEAU to POMMEREUIL 1 man wounded	WM
			Divisional Area. "C" Coy working from Road Junction E. of LE CATEAU to POMMEREUIL filling shell holes and improving drainage	
	29		"A" Coy working from LE CATEAU - BASUEL road to POMMEREUIL improving and repairing. "B" Coy working in all roads in Divisional Area. "C" Coy working from Road Junction E. of LE CATEAU to POMMEREUIL improving drainage and filling shell holes	WM

Army Form C. 2118.

WAR DIARY
or
INTELLIGENCE SUMMARY. PAGE 10
(Erase heading not required.)

Place	Date	Hour	Summary of Events and Information	Remarks and references to Appendices
FRANCE -	OCTOBER 1918			
	29		Roads speaking fit for motor transport traffic	
	30		Batln moved from billets to LE CATEAU Station & Billets in LE CATEAU town	M.M.
	31		"A" Coy improving billets. "B" Coy working on all roads in Boisvaulaires	M.M.
			"C" Coy improving billets and railway crossing	M.M. S.K. S/Capt.

Army Form C. 2118.

WAR DIARY
or
INTELLIGENCE SUMMARY.

(Erase heading not required.) PAGE 11

Instructions regarding War Diaries and Intelligence Summaries are contained in F. S. Regs., Part II. and the Staff Manual respectively. Title pages will be prepared in manuscript. *Nominal role of Officers 3rd Oct 1918*

Place	Date	Hour	Summary of Events and Information				Remarks and references to Appendices
							Present State
UNIT	Appoint	Rank	NAME	UNIT	Appoint	Rank	Name	O	OR
5th Conn of attached Officers	C.O.	Lt Col	HAWKES	M.G.	G.W.				Effective	26	822
	A/2nd in comand	Major	FOLEY		G.R.E.				Attached on Estab	1	1
		Capt	BEARD	M.C.	R.A.M.C.	Medical Officer	Captain	Hill			
		"	HENDRY	W.					Attached for Rations	-	-
		"	DAVIS	C.J.					TOTAL	27	823
		"	JOSEPH	S.G.							
		Lieut	ERRINGTON	E.						8 n	at
		"	KING	F.J.					Lewis Guns		10
	A/Adjt	"	McRAE	T.A.N.							
		"	BAILLIE	H.B.					Draught Horses & Mules		59
		"	ROCHE	M.L.							
		"	MALCOMSON	A.					Pack		12
		"	LOWE	A							
		"	GODFREY	B.J.					Riding		12
		"	HUNTER	V.					Horses		
	2/Lt	"	McNALLY	F.J.					Cobs (Scullery, Mc)		12
Roy Munster Fus		"	HEALY	E.							
Roy. Irish Rifles		"	BELL	W.J.					G.S. Wagons		6
do		"	WYLIE	T.							
		"	CLARE	L.					C.S. Limbers		7
	S/O.A.	"	MEEHAN	T.S.							
		"	HUNTER	H.C.R.					Field Kitchens		3
		"	O'SNES	T.V.							
		"	RICHARDSON	S.A.					Water Carts		3
		"	CORRIGAN	P.M.							
		"	WILLIAMS	J.P.					Maltese Carts		1
	Act/Capt	Lieut	CUNNINGHAM	H.V.					Mess cart		1
									Bicycles		9

Original

CONFIDENTIAL

WAR DIARY

of

5th Bn Royal Irish Regt (Pioneers)

From 1st November 1918 to 30th November 1918

Volume 41

WAR DIARY
INTELLIGENCE SUMMARY.
(Erase heading not required.) Page 1

Army Form C. 2118.

Place	Date	Hour	Summary of Events and Information	Remarks and references to Appendices
FRANCE	NOVEMBER 1918			
	1st		Bn billeted in LE CATEAU. "A" Coy 3 Platoons working maintaining LE CATEAU - BAZUEL Road. "B" Coy resting in billets. "C" Coy making track for infantry from LA FAYT FARM due E. to FONTAINE AU BOIS. G.O.C. inspected Bn at 1500 hours and presented 992 Pte Simpson L. with Military Medal	100mm
	2nd		"A" Coy working on track from FONTAINE Road to LE FAYT FARM. "B" Coy erected Prisoners of War bags S of LE FAYT FARM also working on roads at FONTAINE. "C" Coy making track for infantry from FONTAINE AU BOIS forward in easterly direction towards DRILL GROUND corner as far as situation permitted. Strength Return for Saturday week ending 2nd November 1918. Effective 26 O 832 OR. Admitted to Hospl 7 OR. Ration 270 823 OR. Paid from Hospl 9 OR.	100mm 100mm 100mm
	3rd		"A" and "B" Coys moved billets to Laundry S.E. of LE CATEAU. "C" Coy making tracks and orderlies track connecting D.H.Q. and Brigade H.2 at FONTAINE AU BOIS	100mm

WAR DIARY
INTELLIGENCE SUMMARY.
(Erase heading not required.) Page 2

Army Form C. 2118.

Place	Date	Hour	Summary of Events and Information	Remarks and references to Appendices
FRANCE	NOVEMBER 1918			
	4th		Advanced Bn Hadqrs moved to FONTAINE from LE CATEAU. 'A' and 'B' Coys moved and billeted in FONTAINE. 'C' Coy and rear Bn Hadqrs billeted in POMMEREUIL. 'A' Coy worked from FONTAINE AU BOIS to LANDRECIES Road and on Route de Fontaine. 'B' Coy moved up to MORMAL FOREST with HQ Field Coy R.E. 'C' Coy 1 Platoon continuing track towards DRILL GROUND corner. 1 killed 9 wounded including Platoon Officer. 3 Platoons making road fit for Heavy Transport through LE FAUX - ROSIMBOIS DRILL GROUND CORNER. ROUTE DE LANDRECIES. Bn assembled in FONTAINE and billeted there that night. 'A' Coy worked on	
	5th		ENGLE FONTAINE - LANDRECIES road. 'B' Coy bridging SAMBRE Canal with R.E. also filling mine craters on road RUE DE LANDRECIES. 'C' Coy making two pier bridges at craters on ROUTE DE LANDRECIES	
	6th		Bn moved from FONTAINE AU BOIS to HATCHETTE less Companies working strength who were engaged on roads in Divl Area in FORET de MORMAL 'A' Coy worked on roads in MORMAL FOREST. 'B' Coy maintenance of pontoon bridge at HALT and clearing approach to pontoon bridge at NOYELLES. 'C' Coy draining and repairing road from crater on Route de LANDRECIES to HACHETTE	

Army Form C. 2118.

WAR DIARY
INTELLIGENCE SUMMARY.
(Erase heading not required.) Page 3

Place	Date	Hour	Summary of Events and Information	Remarks and references to Appendices
FRANCE	NOVEMBER - 1918			
	4/5		Bn moved from HATCHETTE to HAUT NOYELLES less 1 Platoon of 'B' Coy. Bn. less 'B' Coy billetted in HAUT NOYELLES. 'B' Coy moved to ST REMY CHAUSSEE. 'A' Coy worked on roads in area between NOYELLES and ST AUBIN. 'B' Coy repair work on Tow Path and approaches to Bridge on SAMBRE CANAL. 'C' Coy helping 4th Field Coy R.E. at deviation at NOYELLES crater also drainage and repairing shell holes on roads HACHETTE NOYELLES MAROILLES LEVAL	
	8th		Bn moved less 'B' Coy from HAUT NOYELLES to MONCEAU ST WAAST. Company working strength moved off for work in Bn area at 0700 hours. Bn (less 'B' Coy) Hd Qrs moved at 0930 hours. 'A' Coy half company filling mine crater, half company clearing debris from railway bridge S of LEVAL. 'B' Coy clearing road through LEVAL and clearing fallen trees on ST AUBIN - MT DOURLERS ROAD. 'C' Coy drawing and filling shell holes on roads REMY CHAUSSEE ST AUBIN DOMPIERRE Road to cross roads	
	9		'A' Coy finished cleaning of railway bridge S of LEVAL. 'B' Coy working on road from ST AUBIN to EKOURSIES also made deviation round crater at DOURLERS. 'C' Coy cleaning block at Railway Bridge Road making road enough for	

Army Form C. 2118.

WAR DIARY
INTELLIGENCE SUMMARY.
(Erase heading not required.) PAGE 4

Instructions regarding War Diaries and Intelligence Summaries are contained in F. S. Regs., Part II. and the Staff Manual respectively. Title pages will be prepared in manuscript.

Place	Date	Hour	Summary of Events and Information	Remarks and references to Appendices
FRANCE	NOVEMBER 1918			
	9		Motor traffic near MONCEAU Road. Two platoons deepened with 4th Field Coy R.E. on Divisional Flying Column.	
			Strength return for week ending Saturday 9th November 1918.	
			Effective 21 O. 459 O.R. Draufted to Hospt. 23 O.R.	
			Ration 22 O. 461 O.R. Rejoined from Hospt. 2 O.R.	
	10		Bn moved from MONCEAU ST WAAST to SEMOUSIES. 16 boy 2 platoons filling in craters on cross Roads at LA SAVATE. "B" boy moved to SARS POTERIES. Work on mine crater at BAUGNIES DIMONT and LES FONTAINE.	
	11		Wire received from 50 Div stating hostilities ceased at 1100 hours. "A" boy one platoon working on bridge at DOURLERS remainder of company within economy. 16 boy loading timber at Quarry. LES BODEUIZ "C" boy repaired Bn at SEMOUSIES	
	12		50 Div Memorial Parade and Presentation of Medals at D.H.Q. DOURLERS. 40 men and 2 officers represented Bn. Lt gl Jackson presented with M.M. by G.O.C. "A" boy 2 platoons working on MAUBEUGE AVESNES Road. 16 boy cleaning and draining road MAUBEUGE AVESNES. "B" boy worked on mine crater at DOURLERS with 416 coy R.E.	

WAR DIARY
INTELLIGENCE SUMMARY

Army Form C. 2118.

PAGE 5

Place	Date	Hour	Summary of Events and Information	Remarks and references to Appendices
FRANCE	NOVEMBER 1918			
	13		"A" Coy 2 Platoons working on MAUBEUGE AVESNES Road rehewing and unhorsing 1 Platoon at Bridge at DOURLERS. "C" Coy cleaning and draining main road DOURLERS - LA SAVATE. "B" Coy worked on road ST AUBIN - DOURLERS	
	14		"A" Coy working on road ST AUBIN - LES BOBOLEZ rehewing and unhorsing. "C" Coy filling craters cleaning and draining road ST AUBIN DOMPIERRE. "B" Coy worked on road from MONT DOURLERS to LA SAVATE FARM	
	15		"A" Coy working on craters at LA SAVATE. "C" Coy rehewing and interior economy. "B" Coy training	
	16		"A" Coy training. Route March in afternoon. "C" Coy filling craters and making same fit for traffic at LA SAVATE. "B" Coy Route March to SARS POTERIES. Strength Return for week ending Saturday 16 November 1918. Effective 24 O 438 OR. Admitted to Hospital 12 OR. Ration 26 O 439 OR. Rejoined from Hospital 4 OR.	
	17		G.O.C. inspected Bn at 1500 hours and presented M.C. to Lieut B.A. Godfrey. Bn paraded hollow square. Transport in rear. C of E, R.C, and Presbyterian services at 0830 hours	

WAR DIARY
or
INTELLIGENCE SUMMARY.

(Erase heading not required.) PAGE 6

Army Form C. 2118.

Place	Date	Hour	Summary of Events and Information	Remarks and references to Appendices
FRANCE	NOVEMBER 1918			
	18		A, B and C Coy training in huts	Nil
	19		A B C Coys Platoon training Coys and Platoon drill Small party "B" Coy salvage work in the area. Recreational training in afternoon	Nil
	20		Half "B" Coy working on crates at LA SAVATE; half Coy training "A" Coy Route march and march discipline. "C" Coy 4 hours training	Nil
	21		"A" Coy and Platoon drill. Half "B" Coy on crates at LA SAVATE, half Coy training "A" Coy Half "B" Coy Route march in morning. Recreational training "C" Coy 4 hours training in afternoon	Nil
	22		"B" Coy 3 Platoons at crates at LA SAVATE. 1 Platoon training. "C" Coy training and recreation in afternoon. "A" Coy training and route march	Nil
	23		"A" Coy "A" Coy on crates at LA SAVATE. "B" Coy 4 hours training. "C" Coy and Platoon drill. Recreational training in afternoon. Strength Return for week ending Saturday 23 November 1918 Effective 24 O 732 OR Admitted to Hospital 9 OR Ration 26 O 733 OR Rejoined from Hospital 11 OR	Nil

WAR DIARY
INTELLIGENCE SUMMARY.

Army Form C. 2118.

(Erase heading not required.) PAGE 7

Place	Date	Hour	Summary of Events and Information	Remarks and references to Appendices
FRANCE	NOVEMBER 1918			
	24		C of E, R C and Non-conformist services held at 8:30 am	
	25		Coy training 4 hours per day and Platoon drill. Classes of education opened	
	26		Coy training. Party of B Coy working at Cemetery DOURLERS. Classes under Education Scheme continued	
	27		30 men 16 Coy working at Cemetery DOURLERS. Coy training & Education Scheme continued	
	28		Party of 16 Company at Cemetery DOURLERS Coy training and Education scheme continued	
	29		Party at Cemetery DOURLERS. Coy training and Route march	
	30		Party at Cemetery DOURLERS. Coy training. Education Scheme continued	
			Strength Return for Saturday week ending 30 November 1918	
			Effective 24 O 949 OR. Admitted to Hospital 11 OR	
			Ration 26 O 948 OR. Rejoined from hospital 19 OR	

Army Form C. 2118.

WAR DIARY
or
INTELLIGENCE SUMMARY.

(Erase heading not required.) Page 8

Instructions regarding War Diaries and Intelligence Summaries are contained in F. S. Regs., Part II. and the Staff Manual respectively. Title pages will be prepared in manuscript. *Effective state of BHQ for 30 November 1916*

Place	Date	Hour	Summary of Events and Information					Remarks and references to Appendices
			Rank	Name	Unit	Appoint	Rank	Name	Present State	
Divisional Office attached BHQ		C.O.	Lt.Col	HAWKES M.C.	G.W.	R.A.M.C.	M.O.	Captain	HILL	J.M°A	Effective	24	O.R. 747
		2nd I/c	Major	EDLEY	G.R.E.	Chaplains Dept	Chaplain	O'FARRELL	P	Attached on Estab	2	1
		Coy. Comd	Capt.	BEARD M.C.	E.C.					Attached for Rations	—	—
		A/Capt.	Lieut	ERRINGTON	E					Total	26	748
		Sig Off	"	ROBIN	A							
		"	"	KING	P.J							
		A/Adjt	"	MCRAE	T.A.N					Riding horses		8
		"	"	BAILLIE	W.D							
		"	"	ROCHE	M.L					Draught horses & mules		53
		"	"	LOWE	A							
		"	"	GODFREY M.C	P.J					Pack " "		12
		"	"	HUNTER	V							
		"	"	GREER	E					Lewis Guns		12
Manchester Regt		2/Lieut		CARNEGIE	R.Y							
Black Watch T.F.		"	"	MCNALLY	F.J					Pack Saddlery (sets)		12
Roy Munster Fus		"	"	HEALY	G							
Roy Irish Rifles		"	"	BELL	W.J					G.S Waggons		6
		"	"	CLARE	J							
		"	"	MEEHAN	J.S					G.S. Limbers		7
		"	"	SIZER M.C	F.M							
		"	"	HUNTER M.C	M.G.R					Field Kitchens		3
		"	"	O'SHEA	J.V							
		"	"	RICHARDSON	C.A					Water Carts		2
		"	"	CORRIGAN	J.H							
		"	"	WILLIAMS	W.P					Mallise Carts		1
		Adjt	A/Capt	CUNNINGHAM	H.U					Mess Cart		1
		Q.M.	Lieut	SCAMMELL	F.W.J.					Bicycles		10

WD 13
Original

87.2
7 sheets

CONFIDENTIAL

— WAR DIARY —

of

5ᵗʰ Bn ROYAL IRISH REGIMENT (Pioneers)

From 1ˢᵗ December 1918 to 31ˢᵗ December 1918.

VOLUME 42

Army Form C. 2118.

WAR DIARY
or
INTELLIGENCE SUMMARY.
(Erase heading not required.) Page 1

Instructions regarding War Diaries and Intelligence Summaries are contained in F. S. Regs., Part II. and the Staff Manual respectively. Title pages will be prepared in manuscript.

Place	Date	Hour	Summary of Events and Information	Remarks and references to Appendices
FRANCE	DECEMBER 1918.			
	1st		C of E and R.C. Church parades at 0830 hours. 149th Brigade formed up on field E of AVESNES-MAUBEUGE Road to see His Majesty the King at 1100 hours. His Majesty the King walked round the Brigade and spoke to several of the men.	C.R.
	2nd		0800 hours, Physical Training and Recreational Games. 0900 hours Coy. Inspection. 0930-1200 hours Coy. Drill, Musketry etc. Small party of C. Coy working at Military Cemetery DOURLERS.	C.R.
	3rd		'C' Coy supplied small party 1 Off. 20 men for work on DOURLERS Cemetery. Remainder of Bn training for 4 hours during morning. Afternoon, Recreational classes for Regular Soldiers continued.	C.R.
	4th		Movement Order received for Bn to move to MARBAIX. Coys. Bathing and Ordinary Economy. Platoon bounds declined. Mum Platoon on arrival of subject. No parades on account of heavy rain.	O.K.
	5th		Bn moved from SEMOUSIES to MARBAIX. Bn being moved off at 0930 hours followed by A.B.C. Coys at 100 yards distance	C.R.
	6th		Coys improving billets. Recreational Training in the afternoon.	C.R.
	7th		Coys paraded for Inspection at 0900 hours. Training & education during morning. Strength Return for week ending 7th December 1918 Effective 23 O 757 O/R Ration 25 O 760 O/R Admitted to Hospital 2 O/R Rejoined from Hospital 13 O/R	C.R.

WAR DIARY
INTELLIGENCE SUMMARY.
(Erase heading not required.) Page 2

Army Form C. 2118.

Place	Date	Hour	Summary of Events and Information	Remarks and references to Appendices
FRANCE	DECEMBER 1918			
	8/5		Bn moved from MAUBAIX to MAROILLES. Bn Hdqrs marched off at 1200 hours followed by A, B, and C Coys at 1/2 hours intervals. Bn Hdqrs billeted in Chateau MAROILLES. "B" Coy football team played "C" Coy 50% Bn M.G.C. in Bn Competition. "B" Coy won by 9 goals to 3.	CR
	9th		Coys paraded for 4 hours training and educational scheme. Officers Riding School commences. All junior officers attend.	CR
	10th		Coys training and education. C.O.'s kit inspection from 1000 hours to 1200 hours. Examination held for regular soldiers for 1st 2nd and 3rd class certificates. Officers Riding School.	CR
	11th		Training and Educational Classes 0800 hours to 1200 hours. Training in billets. Educational Classes.	CR
	12th		Training and Education.	CR
	13		Training and Education. "B" Coy played "C" Coy 1st Wiltshire Regiment Training and Education in Football Competition. "B" Coy 5 goals. 1st Wilts 3 goals.	CR
	14		Divn Inter Coy Football Return for Week Ending Saturday 14th December 1918. Admitted to Hospital 1. O.R. Strength 21 O. 958 O.R. Rejoined from Hospital — Ration 23 O. 959 O.R.	CR

Army Form C. 2118.

WAR DIARY
INTELLIGENCE SUMMARY

(Erase heading not required.) Page 3

Place	Date	Hour	Summary of Events and Information	Remarks and references to Appendices
FRANCE	DECEMBER 1918			
	15th		Struck parade at 0900 hours. Warning order received to move to	C/R
			ST. WAAST LA VALLÉE	
	16th		Training of Regular Soldiers. 50' Div. Warning Order re move cancelled	C/R
	17		Bath. Training. 50' Div. marchroute cancelled	C/R
	18		Training and Education. Warning Order for move to ST WAAST	C/R
			LA VALLÉE received	
	19th		Preparations for move and cleaning billets	
	20		Move to HARGNIES and VIEUX MESNIL. H/r 0900 hours. H.Q. leading.	C/R
			B, A and C Coys followed at 1/2 hour intervals. Arrived HARGNIES	
			1330 hours. B. billeted for night in HARGNIES and VIEUX MESNIL	
	21		Moved to ST WAAST LA VALLÉE. Start 0900 hours H.Q. leading, C, A	C/R
			and B' Coys. Arrived ST. WAAST 1200 hours	
			H.Q. and TRANSPORT billeted in ST WAAST LA VALLÉE	
			A Coy " " BREAUGIES	
			B " " HOUDAIN	
			C " " LA FLAMENGERIE	
			Strength Return for week ending Saturday 21st December 1918	
			Effective 21 O 960 O/R. Admitted to Hospital. 6 O/R	
			Ration 23 O 963 O/R Rejoined from Hospital 1 O/R	

WAR DIARY
INTELLIGENCE SUMMARY

(Erase heading not required.) Page 4

Army Form C. 2118.

Place	Date	Hour	Summary of Events and Information	Remarks and references to Appendices
FRANCE	DECEMBER 1918			
	22		No training. H.Q. Church Parade. R.C. 0800 hours ST. WAAST. Boy Church Parade Optional in French Churches.	CR
	23		No training. Improvement of billets in Both Areas.	CR
	24		No training. Still improving billets. Midnight Mass held in church	CR
			ST. WAAST.	
	25		Observed as a holiday. All boys held mass in churches of villages in which they are billeted at 0800 hours. Sports promoted by boys.	CR
	26		No training. Observed as a holiday.	CR
	27		Training and Education under boy arrangements	CR
	28		Training and Education	CR
			Strength Return for Week Ending Saturday 28 December 1918	
			Effective 20 O 415 O/R Admitted 16 Hospital 13 O/R	
			Ration 22 O 416 O/R Rejoined from Hospital 3 O/R	
	29		Church Parades. 1 Off and 40 O/Ranks A'Coy and 1 Off C Coy proceeded on detachment to COMMEGNIES for work under CRE	CR
	30		Training and Education. Working party still on detachment under CRE	CR
	31		Training and Education.	CR

C A Rickinson 2/Lt

WAR DIARY or INTELLIGENCE SUMMARY

Army Form C. 2118.

Instructions regarding War Diaries and Intelligence Summaries are contained in F. S. Regs., Part II. and the Staff Manual respectively. Title pages will be prepared in manuscript.

Effective List of BnHQ as of 31st Dec 1916. Page 5

Place	Date	Hour	Summary of Events and Information					Remarks and references to Appendices
UNIT	Appt	Rank	Name		Unit	Appt	Rank	Name
In case of attached offr	A/C.O	Major	FOLEY	G.R.E	MRC (USA)	M.O.	Lieut	KANE
		Capt	BEARD	M.C.	E.C.			
		"	HENDRY	W.	Chaplains Dept	Rev Father	Captain	O'FARRELL
		Lieut	DAVIS	C.J.				
		"	KING	F.J.				
		"	BAILLIE	W.B.				
		"	LOWE	A.				
	A/Adjt	"	HUNTER	V.				
		"	CARNEGIE	R.Y.				
		"	HEALY	E.				
		"	BELL	W.J.				
		"	CLARE	J.				
Black Watch		2/Lieut	MEEHAN	J.S.				
Roy Munster R.s		"	STOER	F.M. M.C.				
		"	HUNTER	H.G.R M.C.				
		"	O'SHEA	J.V.				
	T.O	"	RICHARDSON	C.A.				
		"	CORRIGAN	J.H.				

Present State		
	O.R	
L.A. Effective	18	715
Attached on Estab	2	1
P. Attached for Rations	–	–
Total	20	716
Riding Horses		6
Draught Horses & Mules		55
Pack "		17
Lewis Guns		12
Pack Saddlery (sets)		12
G.S Wagons		6
G.S. Limbers		4
Field Kitchens		3
Water Carts		2
Maltese Carts		1
Mess Cart		1
Bicycles		10

Original

CONFIDENTIAL

WAR DIARY

— of —

5th Bn ROYAL IRISH RGT. (Pioneers)

From 1st January 1919 to 31st January 1919

VOLUME 43

Army Form C. 2118.

WAR DIARY
— or —
INTELLIGENCE SUMMARY.
(Erase heading not required.) Page 1

Instructions regarding War Diaries and Intelligence Summaries are contained in F. S. Regs., Part II. and the Staff Manual respectively. Title pages will be prepared in manuscript.

Place	Date	Hour	Summary of Events and Information	Remarks and references to Appendices
FRANCE	1st January 1919		Observed as holiday. Church Parade in morning.	7/F
	2nd		Training and Education. Football match at HOUDAIN. B Coy v A. KRRC. Result 1 B Coy 1 KRRC 0.	7/F
	3rd		Training and Education. Detachment from C Coy 1 Off 30 O/Ranks proceeded to WARGNIES. LE PETIT for work under instructions of C RE	7/F
	4th		Training and Education. Strength Return for Week ending Saturday 4 January 1919. Effective 19 O 413 O/R. Admitted to hospital 3 O/R. Ration 21 O 414 O/R. Rejoins from hospital — 1	7/F
	5th		Church parade. R C 0800 hours ST.WAAST. C of E 0900 hours ST.WAAST.	7/F
	6th		Training and Education. Football match 1st round Divisional Competition. B Coy v 250 Bde R.F.A. Result 5 R.I. Regt (?) 3 250 Bde R.F.A. 3	7/F
	7th		Training and Education. Replay of yesterday's football match at SAULTAIN. Result 6th Bn Roy I Regt 4. 250 Bde R.F.A. 0.	7/F
	8th		Training and Education. Final of Div Competition. B Coy v 13" Scottish Horse. Result B Coy 1. Scottish Horse 0	7/F
	9th		Training and Education.	7/F
	10th		Training and Education. 2nd Round Div Competition. Salta v 251 Bde R.F.A at HOUDAIN. Result Salta 3. 251 Bde R.F.A 2.	7/F

WAR DIARY
of
INTELLIGENCE SUMMARY.
(Erase heading not required.) Page 2

Army Form C. 2118.

Place	Date	Hour	Summary of Events and Information	Remarks and references to Appendices
	11"		Training and Education. "A" Coy detachment returned from SOMMEGNIES	7K
			Strength return for week ending Saturday January 11, 1919	
			Effective 17 O 403 O/R	
			Ration 19 O 404 O/R	
			Church Parades R.C. at 0900 hours C of E at 1100	
	12"		hours at BAVAI. Admitted to Hospital 1 O/R	7K
			Rejoined from Hospital 3 O/R	
	13"		Training and Education.	7K
	14"		Training and Education.	7K
	15"		Training and Education.	7K
	16"		Training and Education. Football. Bn v 50 Div R.E. 3 a round Bn O. R.E.O	7K
			Div Competition.	
	17"		Training and Education.	7K
	18"		Training and Education.	7K
			Strength Return for Week Ending Saturday January 18, 1919	
			Effective 20 O 696 O/R Admitted to Hospital 5 O/R	
			Ration 22 O 697 O/R Rejoined from Hospital 7 O/R	
			Church Parades R.C. Mass at ST WAAST Ch at 0900 hours C of E	
	19"		Service at BAVAI at 1100 hours. Football in afternoon "B" Coy of Battn	7K
			v "B" Coy of E Surrey Regt (18 Div). B Coy S. E. Surreys 2	
			Replay of match v R.E. Result R.E. 2 Batt 1	

WAR DIARY
or
INTELLIGENCE SUMMARY.

Army Form C. 2118.

Page 3

Place	Date	Hour	Summary of Events and Information	Remarks and references to Appendices
	21		Training and Education. 2 Off and 49 O/Ranks proceeded to U.K. for purpose of demobilisation	T/R
	22		Rehearsal of presentation of colours in BAVAI with 6 Innis. and 4th Wilts.	T/R
	23		Training and Education	T/R
	24		Training and Education	T/R
	25		Training and Education. Return for Week Ending Saturday 25 January 1919. Strength Effective 19 O 641 O/R Admitted to Hospt 4 O/R Ration 21 O 642 O/R Rejoined from Hospt 5 O/R	T/R
	26		Church Parades. R.C. Mass at HOUDAIN and ST WAAST and C of E Service at BAVAI at 1100 hours. FLAMENGRIES at 0900 hours V 2 N Field Ambulance 2nd round Corps Competition Football B Coy V 2 N Field Ambulance 3 B Coy 1.	T/R
	27		Training and Education	T/R
	28		Training and Education	T/R
	29		Training and Education	T/R
	30		Training and Education	T/R
	31		Training and Education	T/R

W.h. H.w.H. RLVA
Capt

Army Form C. 2118.

WAR DIARY
INTELLIGENCE SUMMARY

(Erase heading not required.) Page 1

Instructions regarding War Diaries and Intelligence Summaries are contained in F. S. Regs., Part II. and the Staff Manual respectively. Title pages will be prepared in manuscript. Effective State B/o for 31 Jan 1919

Place	Date	Hour	Appoint	Rank	Names		Unit	Appoint	Rank	Name	Unit
Leave of att			C.O	Lt.Col	HAWKES	G.M.		M.O	Lieut	KANE	L.R.
2nd in cond			2nd in com	Major	FOLEY	G.R.G.					
			Capt.	HENDRY	W.		Rev Father	Captain	O'FARRELL	R.
					DAVIS	C.J.	Chaplains Dept				
		A/		ERRINGTON	E.						
					BRILLIS	W.B.					
			Lieut	ROBIN	A.						
Leave			"	ROCHE	M.L.						
			"	LOWE	A.						
			"	GODFREY	Mc P.J.						
			"	HUNTER	V.						
			"	HEALY	E.						
			"	BELL	W.J.						
			"	CLARE	J.						
			"	MEEHAN	J.S.						
Roy Munster			"	STOER	Mc F.M.						
Fus			"	HUNTER	H.G.R.						
		Leave	"	O'SHER	J.V.						
			"	RICHARDSON	C.R.						
			"	CORRIGAN	J.H.						
			"	WILLIAMS	W.R.						
		Adjt	Capt	CUNNINGHAM	H.J.						
		Q.M.	Lt	SCAMMELL	A.W.J.						

Present State

	O.	O.R.
Effective	21	641
Attached on Estab	2	1
" for Rations	—	—
TOTAL	23	642

Riding Horses	9
Draught Horses & Mules	53
Pack	13
Lewis Guns	12
Pack Saddlery (sets)	12
G S Wagons	6
G S Limbers	4
Field Kitchens	3
Water Carts	2
Maltese "	1
Mess "	1
Bicycles	10

CONFIDENTIAL

WAR DAIRY

of

5ᵗʰ Bⁿ ROYAL IRISH REGᵗ (PIONEERS)

FROM 1ˢᵗ FEBRUARY 1919 to 28ᵗʰ FEBRUARY 1919

VOLUME 44

Army Form C. 2118.

WAR DIARY
of
INTELLIGENCE SUMMARY.

(Erase heading not required.) PAGE 1

Instructions regarding War Diaries and Intelligence Summaries are contained in F. S. Regs., Part II. and the Staff Manual respectively. Title pages will be prepared in manuscript.

Place	Date	Hour	Summary of Events and Information	Remarks and references to Appendices
FRANCE ST WAAST-LA-VALLEE	February 1919			
	1st		Training & Education – Strength Return for week ending Saturday Feby 1st 1919. Officers – 21 ORs – 641 Admitted to hospital nil. Rations – 23 642 Rejoined from hospital one.	Nil
	2nd		Holiday – Church Service – RC Mass at 0900 hours in Church ST WAAST for BHQ & Transport. RC Mass at 0800 hours at HOUDAIN for 'A' & 'B' Coys. C of E Service at BAVAI at 1100 hours	Nil
	3rd		Training & Education – Medical Inspection and Completing of disposal forms of 20 men for day commenced.	Nil
	4th		Training & Education. Notification received that no men who joined the Colours after 1st Jany 1916 to be demobilised.	Nil
	5th		Training & Education in morning – Football in afternoon 2/Lt H Corrigan Cpl Hands demobilised	Nil
	6th		Training & Education	Nil
	7th		Training & Education – 9 men left Unit to proceed for disposal	Nil
	8th		Training & Education – Football Match 'B' Coy V 8th R. Scots 8Coy 3 R 0 1 2 Men left unit for disposal Strength Return for week ending Saturday Feby 8th 1919. Officers – 18 ORs – 574 Admitted to hospital Three Rations – 20 575 Rejoined from Hospital nil	Nil

D. D. & L., London, E.C.
Wt. W1771/M2/31 750,000 5/17 Sch. 52 Forms/C1118/14
(A804)

WAR DIARY

INTELLIGENCE SUMMARY.

(Erase heading not required.) PAGE 2

Army Form C. 2118.

Place	Date	Hour	Summary of Events and Information	Remarks and references to Appendices
FRANCE ST.WAAST-LA-VALLEE	9th		Holiday. Church Parade. R.C. Mass at ST WAAST. LA.FLAMENGERIE and HOUDAIN. C of E Voluntary Service at BAVAI at 1100 hours	Nil
	10th		Training & Education in Morning. Recreation in afternoon. Major F.R.E. Joly left 9th for Demobilisation	Nil
	11th		Training & Education. 1 Man left Unit for Disposal	Nil
	12th		Training & Education. Party of 4 Officers and 25 O/Ranks went to NAMUR to see Battle Ground	Nil
	13th		Training & Education. 18 Men left Unit for Disposal	Nil
	14th		Training & Education. Recreation in afternoon. 6 men left Unit for Disposal - Capt W. Hendry & Lieut A. Lowe left Unit for Demobilisation	Nil
	15th		Training & Education. 31 Men left Unit for Disposal	
			Strength Return for week ending Saturday 15th February 1919	
			Os ORs	
			Effective 16 558 Admitted to Hospital One	
			Ration 18 359 Returned from Hospital Two	Nil
	16th		Holiday. Church Parade. R.C. Mass at ST WAAST, HOUDAIN, LAFLAMENGRIE C of E Voluntary Service at BAVAI at 1100 hours. 8 Men left Unit for Disposal	Nil

WAR DIARY

INTELLIGENCE SUMMARY

(Erase heading not required.) PAGE 3

Army Form C. 2118.

Place	Date	Hour	Summary of Events and Information	Remarks and references to Appendices
ST MAAST LA VALLEE	17th		All men for Army of Occupation formed into 1 Company and billeted in BRY. Remainder of Bttn evacuated HOUDAIN & LA FLAMENGRIE and concentrated in ST WAAST	Nil
	18th		Training & Education – Recreation	Nil
	19th		Training & Education – Recreation	Nil
	20th		Training & Education – Recreation	Nil
			1 man left Unit to disperse	
			Lieut Kane M.O. % joined Southampton F.A.	Nil
	21st		Intimation received that Bttn to entrain on 26th inst at LE QUESNOY for 2nd Army on the Rhine.	
			Training & Education – Recreation. 17 men left Unit to disperse	
			Arrangements made to medically inspect and complete forms for all demobilisable men before Bttn entrains	Nil
	22nd		Training & Education in morning – Recreation in afternoon	
			Strength Return for week ending February 22nd 1919	
			O.R.S 513	
			Officers 14	
			Ration 15 514	
			Admitted to Hospital – one	
			Reported from do – nil	Nil

WAR DIARY of INTELLIGENCE SUMMARY.

(Erase heading not required.) PAGE A

Army Form C. 2118.

Place	Date	Hour	Summary of Events and Information	Remarks and references to Appendices
ST WAAST - LA - VALLÉE	23rd		Notification received that all releasable men will be transferred to 6th Royal Inniskilling Inniskilling pending demobilisation. Telegram received cancelling move until 27th relating Bttn will form 2nd (Light) Division at ROMMERSKIRCHEN.	NJC
			9s Men left bttn to proceed for dispersal	
			Church Parades — Voluntary RC Service at 09.00 hours in Church ST WAAST	NJC
	24th		Schooling and Training in morning — Men employed cleaning Billets in afternoon	NJC
	25th		3 Offrs 4 244 ORanks left Bttn to join 6th Royal Inniskilling Inniskillings	NJC
			Brig Genl Robinson inspected Party Training behind 2/Lt Whelan & 2/Lt W.S. Mathews left Bttn to proceed 2UK early terms of A.F. S650	NJC NJC
	26th		Men employed cleaning billets and preparing for move	
	27th		29th Left ST WAAST by Mack's lorry at 1100 hours and entrained at LE QUESNOY at 3.30 hours. Strength 9 Offrs 121 ORanks - 7 Riding Horses 2 HD Horses	
			Remainder of Bttn joined 6th Inniskilling Fusiliers and remainder of animals handed to Mobile Veterinary Section - All wagons entrained with Bttn	NJC
	28th		On the train passing through Belgium 2 hours halt Repas at MONS, NAMUR, HUY, and VERVIERS	NJC

W. Cunningham Cpt.

WAR DIARY
INTELLIGENCE SUMMARY

Army Form C. 2118.

Effective State of Bn. for 28th Feby 1919.   PAGE 5

Place	Date	Hour	APPT	RANK	NAME		UNIT	APPT	RANK	NAME		PRESENT STATE	Remarks and references to Appendices
UNIT			APPT	RANK	NAME								
In comd of 1st bn			C.O.	LTCOL	HAWKES MC	G.W.	CHAPLAINS DEPT	REV. FATHER	CAPTAIN	O'FARRELL	P	EFFECTIVE 8 121	
												ATTACHED on ESTAB 1 -	
			CAPT		BEARD	E.C.						" for RATIONS -	
			"		DAVIS	C.J.						TOTAL 9 121	
			LIEUT		BELL	W.J.							
			"		CLARE	J						RIDING HORSES	7
			"		O'SHEA	J.V.						DRAUGHT "	2
			2 "		RICHARDSON	C.A.						LEWIS GUNS	12
			ADJT CAPT		CUNNINGHAM	H.N.						PACK SADDLERY SETS	12
												G.S. WAGONS	6
												G.S. LIMBERS	7
												FIELD KITCHENS	3
												WATER CARTS	2
												MALTESE "	1
												MESS "	1
												BICYCLES	9